—| *The* |—
CHRISTIAN
FAMILY
TOOLBOX

The
CHRISTIAN
FAMILY
TOOLBOX

52
Benedictine
Activities
for the Home

DAVID ROBINSON

A *Crossroad* Book
The Crossroad Publishing Company
New York

The Crossroad Publishing Company
481 Eighth Avenue, New York, NY 10001

Copyright © 2001 by David Robinson

Printed in the United States of America

Library of Congress Cataloging-in-Publication Data

Robinson, David, 1957-
    The Christian family toolbox : 52 Benedictine activities for the home / David Robinson.
        p. cm.
    Includes bibliographical references.
    ISBN 0-8245-1958-2 (alk. paper)
    1. Family – Religious life. 2. Benedict, Saint, Abbot of Monte Cassino. Regula. I. Title.
    BV4526.2 .R59 2001
    249 – dc21

                               2001001974

1   2   3   4   5   6   7   8   9   10   06   05   04   03   02   01

To my family cloister,
Trina, my best friend and wife,
and our three sons,
Jonathan, Stefan, and Thomas,
who have shown me the way
"to the loftier summits"

CONTENTS

Introduction

THE GARDEN PATH

You have made known to me the path of life; you will fill me with joy in your presence, with eternal pleasures at your right hand.
— Psalm 16:11

See how God's love shows us the way of life. Clothed then with faith and the performance of good works, let us set out on this way, with the Gospel for our guide.
— The Rule of St. Benedict, Prologue[1]

My favorite Vincent Van Gogh painting, "First Steps," portrays a humble family garden in early summer. In the background we see a sun-washed cottage and a flowering fruit tree. An open garden gate welcomes us onto the garden path. At the center of the painting, a tender family drama unfolds. The father has set aside his hoe to kneel down and receive his little girl with outstretched arms; the mother bends over to support their infant daughter as she reaches out to take her "first steps."

Like Van Gogh, Benedict of Nursia (480–547) pictures family life in the Rule of St. Benedict as a gated enclosure, a *cloister*, within which we find spiritual growth in a loving family. This growth doesn't happen by chance, but only as we take "first steps" along God's garden paths into the arms of our heavenly Father. At the heart of Benedictine wisdom we find a *family cloister*, life together within the enclosure of God's love, guided by God's Word, under the loving leadership of our heavenly Father.

I am not a monk. I'm married, have three teenage sons, and work full-time as a Presbyterian pastor. As a pastor and a man of faith in God, I am indebted to the Benedictine cloister for spiritual renewal and deepening of my spiritual life in Christ. During the past sixteen years I've made regular prayer retreats at Benedictine and Trappist monasteries.

Within the embrace of the cloister I've enjoyed sitting at the feet of saints, learning from the wise spiritual guides who have traveled this path before me. Over the past two decades, at abbeys in five different states, I've developed friendships with monastic brothers and sisters who have shown me the "tools" of the cloister. I find myself curiously attracted to the way monks live.

Benedictine monks practice their spiritual life daily within the cloister, in the presence of their brothers or sisters. They are family. Recently, I was at the Trappist abbey near Lafayette, Oregon, talking with a friend monk, Brother Martin. He had just finished reading my previous book, *The Family Cloister: Benedictine Wisdom for the Home*,[2] and told me I needed to come live a few months in the cloister and get the true story of what monks are really like. Without intending to do so, I painted an overly pretty picture of Benedictine monastic life. According to my monastic friends, daily life in the monastery is not glamorous. Read Thomas Merton and you discover the same truth:

> As long as we are on earth, the love that unites us will bring us suffering by our very contact with one another, because

this love is the resetting of a Body of broken bones. Even saints cannot live with saints on this earth without some anguish, without some pain at the differences that come between them.[3]

Life together in a family is hard work. There are no short-cuts to true community. The only way into true community is through the daily tools and tasks of living together, being real before one another and before God. Benedictine monks have been living this way for the better part of fifteen hundred years. Benedictine monasteries are families of compassion, spiritual maturity, and growth.

Where does this spiritual growth come from? Monks employ tools from God's toolbox, the Bible, as they walk daily upon God's garden paths of prayer, study, and manual labor. Monasteries are self-supporting, hard-working communities. Monks daily break a sweat by their manual labor to support both their own community and to provide charitable gifts to the needy beyond the walls of the monastery. The brothers I've spoken with over the past two decades are not only industrious, but also delightfully down-to-earth people who keep pointing me Godward.

Through commitment to prayer and study, monks root themselves in Christ and overflow with spiritual fruitfulness. Through their ministry of hospitality, I continue to receive an invitation to join them on these garden paths of prayer, study, and work. I always come away from my monthly retreats to the monastery refreshed in my spiritual life, more in love with God, and more able to love my brothers and sisters in need.

This is the enduring legacy of the Rule of St. Benedict. Written fifteen hundred years ago by Benedict of Nursia, in the early sixth century, the Rule as practiced and lived by monastics today continues to mature people in their love for God and their love for one another. Benedict wrote a practical manual, or "toolbox," for family living. Benedictine monks continue to live by the principles and guidelines of this manual on a daily basis.

Drawing upon this wise family guidebook, *The Family Cloister: Benedictine Wisdom for the Home* explores Benedict's Rule to unearth the riches found there and offer them to parents for their holy calling of raising children. As I wrote in *The Family Cloister*, "According to Benedict, the good way for the family lies beyond the garden gate, within the family cloister. In the pages ahead I hope to reflect with you upon family life in the light of Scripture and Benedict's Rule. I follow the Rule chapter by chapter through this work, drawing upon Benedict's wisdom, applying his insights on communal living to family life today."[4]

The present book, *The Christian Family Toolbox: 52 Benedictine Activities for the Home,* is a companion guide, a hands-on activity book for use by parents with their children, or grandparents with grandchildren, in the daily adventure of family life together.

Many people have added tools to our family toolbox. I give thanks for our families, the Robinsons and the Hudsons, for their love and influence on our children throughout their lives. Several faith families have also richly blessed us, including the people of Columbia Presbyterian Church, Vancouver, Washington, and the people of Smith Memorial Presbyterian Church, Fairview, Oregon, during the early days of our parenting; our friends with the Presbyterian Student Fellowship at Middle Tennessee State University, Murfreesboro, Tennessee, during our middle parenting years; the brothers at Our Lady of Guadalupe Trappist Abbey, Lafayette, Oregon; and since 1993, our church family at Community Presbyterian Church, Cannon Beach, Oregon. I thank them for their prayers and their unconditional love and support; they shared

with us the grace and peace of Jesus Christ in abundance. I grate-
fully acknowledge John Eagleson, editor, and Gwendolin Herder,
publisher, as well as the entire Crossroad publishing family.

Whenever we plant a small backyard garden, I find wise gardeners and get their green thumb insights into how to grow a healthy
garden and deal with common garden problems. I'm no expert on
family life and even less an expert when it comes to monastic life.
In both realms, I'm an amateur. Someone reminded me recently
that the word "amateur" comes from the Latin word for "love."
An amateur is simply a person who does something for the love of
it, not for pay or profit. For nineteen years, we've experienced the
daily joys and challenges of raising children simply for the love of
it. For the past seventeen years, I've gotten away from my family
to enjoy regular prayer retreats at Benedictine monasteries for the
love of it.

The Christian Family Toolbox draws upon the wisdom of Benedict in his Rule, offering ideas and activities for families who want
to grow deeper in their life together. I've gathered these activities
under Benedictine principles found in the Rule: family design, spirituality, discipline, health, life together, hospitality, and growth.
Through this collection of activities, I invite you to walk the garden paths of Benedictine spirituality. My hope for you and your
family is that you will encounter God along these garden paths,
discover tools for your family life, and grow more fruitful in your
family garden, as you and your children journey together further
into the family cloister.

Chapter One

ACTIVITIES FOR FAMILY DESIGN

The love of Christ must come before all else.

— The Rule of St. Benedict, chap. 4

A game our children played during their elementary years was "The Measuring Game." Equipped with only a ruler, a yardstick, or a tape measure, they journeyed from room to room, conquering their domestic world with the tools of measurement.

Try this with your elementary age children. Give them a ruler and a tape measure and have them make a floor plan of your home with measurements written for each room. Provide them with graph paper, pencils, and measuring tools.

After they've come up with your current home design, ask them what they think would be the ideal floor plan for your family home. Several years ago, we began to look at floor plans for a new home. We asked our children to help in the design, room by room. We gave them a ruler and graph paper and turned them loose. They came up with spiral staircases into exclusive hideaways, circular racetracks, whole rooms dedicated to Legos, and many other creative child-oriented concepts. Some of these made it into our final blueprints.

Benedict gave Western civilization such a gift: a simple Rule with which successive generations of children could measure their life and discover more of God's blueprints for family life together. The Rule of St. Benedict, a brief guidebook of seventy-three chapters, defined what communal life was to look like for God's children living in the monastery.

The activities in chapter 1 provide your family a few measuring tools to assess your current family life design and to make changes in the way you design your family life together. These are taken from the Rule of St. Benedict, adapted for your family, drawing upon *The Family Cloister: Benedictine Wisdom for the Home*. My hope is that you will find some of these activities helpful during your daily or weekly family time together and, through trying out some of these ideas, your family design will grow into and become more of the kind of family you've always yearned for.

✝ Activity 1: The Family Cloister Questionnaire

Benedict opens his monastic guidebook with a description of four types of monks: Life-Together monks; Life-Apart monks; Life-without-Rules monks; Life-on-the-Move monks. In *The Family Cloister,* I explore the creative tensions all families face within these four family types: the tension between community and individuality, participation and separation, discipline and freedom, and stability and mobility.

At a family meeting, ask your family to write down (if your children are of the writing age) and discuss what kind of family life you currently experience. We've found that we improve our family discussions when we ask every family member to listen to others without making any negative comments about their viewpoint.

Family Cloister Questionnaire

What do you like most about your family right now? List five favorite family qualities.

1.

2.

3.

4.

5.

What do you like least about your family now? List five family traits you would like to change.

1.

2.

3.

4.

5.

If you have older children, have a family discussion about these questions:

✠ How do we balance our individual life and our family community life?

✛ How do you feel about the amount of time that we're together and apart?

✛ What do you think about freedom and discipline in this family?

✛ Do you feel that our family is too much in a rut or too much on the go?

✛ Activity 2: A Survey Just for Parents

In chapter 2 of the Rule of St. Benedict, we find these challenging words about leadership in a monastic community:

> *To be worthy of the task of governing a monastery, the prioress and abbot must always remember what their title signifies and act accordingly. The prioress or abbot is believed to hold the place of Christ in the monastery. Therefore, a prioress or abbot must never teach or decree or command anything that would deviate from God's instructions.* (RB, 2)

I believe that God calls parents into a spiritual role, to hold the place of Christ in the home. Below, I offer a parenting survey, a tool to assess how we're doing in our spiritual calling from God. The questions are drawn from "Qualities of the Abbot," in chapter 2 of the Rule of St. Benedict.

Parenting Survey

Respond to the statements about parenting below (true or false, agree or disagree), and then share with your spouse or a close friend your ideas about parenting in each of these areas.

1. I view my life as a parent as a spiritual calling from God.

2. I spend at least five minutes of "genuine encounter" time daily with my child.

3. I raise my children *more by example than by words*.

4. I treat my children as precious gifts from God.

5. In raising my children, I believe I've *undertaken the care of souls for whom [I] must give an account*.

6. As a parent, I *show equal love to everyone and apply the same discipline to all*.

7. I'm still learning and growing as a parent and see parenting as lifelong learning.

8. I discipline my children fairly with moderation and mercy.

9. I look for and celebrate the signs of spiritual growth in my children.

10. I take time daily to enjoy the adventure of the spiritual calling of raising children.

✚ Activity 3: *Great Family Meetings*

Benedictine communities meet weekly to discuss their common life in light of the Rule. As Benedict instructs, *As often as anything important is to be done in the monastery, the prioress or abbot shall call the whole community together and explain what the business is* (RB, 3).

Over the years, we've enjoyed regular family meetings, and in the process, improved the quality of our family life. As our children have grown into their teenage years and become active in various school events, we've often missed family meetings. We still try to meet at least once a month and follow the familiar pattern for a family meeting. Here is an outline for a great family meeting:

Call the Family Together

✤ Set a regular time to meet together as a family. Make this time a family priority. Everyone is expected to show up and participate.

✤ Plan meetings, in style and length, with the age level of your children in mind.

Start the Family Meeting

✤ Play a favorite family song to announce the family meeting is about to begin. You may want to begin the meeting with dessert.

✤ Open the family meeting with one person in the family offering a prayer of thanks to God.

✤ Share family stories from the week, heaping encouragement and praise on family members.

Deal with Family Issues and Problems

✤ Discuss family issues and problems, asking for ideas on how to improve family life.

✤ Write down ideas and decisions in a family journal.

✤ Encourage everyone, even the youngest, to participate according to their ability.

✠ Make decisions by family consensus if possible, though parents always have final say.

Close with a Brief Family Devotion

✠ Have one member of the family light a candle, one used only for family meetings.

✠ Read a Bible story together: begin by reading through one of the Gospels, story by story.

✠ Hold hands in a circle and pray together, giving thanks to God for specific blessings.

✠ Follow up on any decisions you've made, reminding children about them through the week.

✠ Activity 4: Make a Family "Toolbox"

✠ Find a shoe box and wrap it up with colored pictures of tools taken out of a catalogue or tool magazine. Or find a small toolbox.

✠ Write out the fifty-two family "tools of love" (see below) on 3 x 5 cards and place them in the "toolbox."

✠ Every week at a family meeting or meal together, ask one family member to draw out a "tool."

✠ Look up the Scripture verse connected with this particular tool.

✠ Spend the week learning more of how to use that tool, putting it into action.

✛ Report the following week about a way you used this tool during the week.

Fifty-Two Family Tools of Love

In *The Family Cloister*, I took the seventy-three Benedictine *tools for good works* (RB, 4) and adapted them for the home.[5]

1. Love God with all your heart, soul, and strength (Luke 10:27).

2. Love one another as Christ loves you (John 13:34).

3. Clothe yourself with compassion, kindness, humility, gentleness, and patience (Colossians 3:12).

4. Develop the habit of giving and the spirit of gratitude (2 Corinthians 9:7).

5. Practice honesty (Mark 10:19).

6. Respect others (1 Peter 2:17).

7. Live by the Golden Rule: "Do to others what you would have them do to you" (Matthew 7:12).

8. Follow Christ with your hearts, minds, and bodies (Matthew 16:24).

9. Keep the desires of your bodies in check by practicing fasting (Isaiah 58:6–7).

10. Care for the needy in your community (Matthew 6:2–3).

11. Clothe the poor (Matthew 25:36).

12. Visit the sick (Matthew 25:36).

13. Help out those who are troubled (Romans 12:20).

14. Comfort the grieving (2 Corinthians 1:3–4).

15. Reject worldliness (Luke 4:5–8).

16. Bridle your anger and temper (Ephesians 4:26).

17. Weed out any deceit in your hearts (Matthew 5:8).

18. Practice true peacemaking (Matthew 5:9).

19. Live a life of charity (Ephesians 5:1–2).

20. Speak the truth in love with your hearts and lips (Ephesians 4:15).

21. Practice kindness (1 Thessalonians 5:15).

22. Do not injure anyone, but patiently endure injuries (Matthew 5:39).

23. Return blessing for cursing (Romans 12:14).

24. Love your enemies by praying for them and seeking to serve them (Matthew 5:44).

25. Do not insult those who insult you, but rather speak well of them (1 Peter 3:9).

26. Be willing to suffer for the sake of justice and truth (Matthew 5:10).

27. Live moderately with regard to drink, food, sleep, and work (Titus 1:7–8).

28. Combat procrastination by making a list of what needs to be done this week (Romans 12:11–12).

29. Offer hospitality (Romans 12:13).

30. Avoid complaining and slander (Ephesians 4:31).

31. Be quick to encourage and build up one another (Ephesians 4:29).

32. Put your highest trust in God (Psalm 62).

33. Give thanks to God for the good you see in your life (Psalm 100).

34. Take responsibility for the sin you see in your life (Psalm 51).

35. Live with regard to eternity (Romans 6:22–23).

36. Live fully; face death (Philippians 1:21).

37. Keep watch over your actions and thoughts (Matthew 26:41).

38. Give up all your anxieties to God (1 Peter 5:7).

39. Remove obscenity, trash talk, and destructive speech from the home (Ephesians 5:4).

40. Enjoy time daily reading the Bible (Colossians 3:16).

41. "Be joyful always; pray continually; give thanks in all circumstances" (1 Thessalonians 5:16–18).

42. Confess your sins to God daily (Psalm 32).

43. Resist the destructive desires of the flesh (Galatians 5:16).

44. Submit to those in authority over you (Romans 13:1).

45. Strive to live a holy life (Romans 12:1).

46. Put your faith in God into action (Matthew 7:24–25).

47. Cherish God and God's way of life more than possessions and passions (Matthew 6:33).

48. Honor the elderly and care for the young (James 1:27).

49. Make peace with your opponent, as soon as possible, if at all possible (Romans 12:18).

50. Live in the shadow of God's mercy (Psalm 91:1–2).

51. Go to sleep every night with a clear conscience (Psalm 4:
    4–8).

52. Begin each new day with prayer to God (Psalm 5:1–3).

✛ Activity 5: Trust Walk

Here's an enjoyable activity I've used for years to help teenagers
to learn to follow verbal directions and develop trust. It's what I
call a "trust walk." Benedict writes of such a walk in his chapter
on obedience:

> *The first step of humility is unhesitating obedience, which comes
> naturally to those who cherish Christ above all.... Such people
> as these immediately put aside their own concerns.... With ready
> steps of obedience, they follow the voice of authority in their
> actions.* (RB, 5)

The Benedictine view of obedience is stepping along a pathway,
following the directions of someone wiser than I am. Obedience
involves my whole self, placing my life into the trust of another:
a parent, a sibling, a family member, a work partner, a friend, or
God. Obedience involves taking a risk. Obedience is an invitation
to trust.

Going for a Family Trust Walk

✛ Using long socks or scarves as blindfolds, pair up the family:
  one blindfolded and one able to see.

✤ Explain the rules: the leader cannot touch the blind partner, but only give verbal instructions: Three steps forward, Stop, Turn left, four steps forward . . . and so on.

✤ Encourage leaders to go slowly and cautiously, offering warnings when the blind partner is about to get into danger. Encourage followers to listen and trust their guides, doing what they say.

✤ Select a path for your trust walk: this could include going outside into the backyard, up and down stairs, through various rooms, even around the block.

✤ When one pair reaches the end of the trust path, switch roles.

✤ After every family member has been both a leader and a follower, sit together as a family and share your feelings and insights on trust, obedience, and following directions.

✤ Activity 6: *Quiet Mouse Game*

Invite God's gift of silence into your family life by playing the Quiet Mouse Game. We play this game in the car on long trips when our kids have talked nonstop for too long. Though especially enjoyed by younger children, the Quiet Mouse Game can be played at any age with delightful results.

✤ Begin the game by declaring: "Time to play the Quiet Mouse Game!"

✤ Tell the family how long the game will last: five minutes, until we reach a rest area, until we get home.

✤ Everyone stops talking and stops making any noise; everyone becomes as "quiet as a mouse."

✤ Continue for the designated period of time.

✤ If you are riding in a car, focus your attention on the scenery and on the imagination.

✤ Observe colors and shapes, unusual details otherwise missed because you were talking. Store these away to share with the family when the game is over.

✤ Ring a little bell or beep an alarm watch when the game is up.

✤ Have family members share their observations or their favorite thought or sight while playing the game.

Benedict invites us into God's gift of silence when he writes, *there are times when good words are to be left unsaid out of esteem for silence* (RB, 6). Besides giving parents an occasional break from the chatter of children cooped up in a car for several hours, the Quiet Mouse Game teaches children to rely upon senses and God-given abilities other than just speech to connect with their world and with one another. This game can be an effective means of creative discipline during road-trip fights as well.

✤ Activity 7: Twelve Flower Pots of Humility

The word "humility" comes from an ancient word for "good earth," *humus*. Humility simply means being earthy, unpretentious, true to whom God made me. This comes about as I die to my false self by being planted in God's love and spring to new life as the person God wants me to become. Benedict describes this process as a ladder with twelve rungs.

> *If we want to reach the highest summit of humility, if we desire to attain speedily that exaltation in heaven to which we climb by*

*the humility of this present life, then by our ascending actions we
must set up that ladder. . . . We descend by exaltation and ascend
by humility. Now the ladder erected is our life on earth, and if
we humble our hearts the Lord will raise it to heaven.* (RB, 7)

To teach your family the twelve Benedictine qualities of humility,
try this activity. Plant twelve flower pots, each with a different
aspect of God's holy work of humility.

Materials

flower pots: small clay pots, washed pint milk cartons, or
plastic cups

packets of flower seeds

humus, good earth, potting soil, or some topsoil from your yard

water

twelve sticks and twelve 3 x 5 cards

Activity

Fill all twelve pots with earth. Plant the seeds, each packet in
a different pot. Write out the twelve Qualities of Humility (see
below) on the lower half of a 3 x 5 card. Fold the cards and staple
them to the top of each stick. Place a stick in every pot. Water
lightly and place the flower pots in a sunny place. Remember to
water the flowers. Enjoy the blossoming goodness of God through
the good earth of humility.

The Twelve Qualities of Humility

1. *Faith:* Focus your eyes on God.

2. *Love:* Love God's will more than your own.

3. *Submission:* Submit your life to those in authority over you.

4. *Endurance:* Put up with afflictions without complaining.

5. *Confession:* Confess your wrongs humbly to another.

6. *Joy:* Be content with the simple life.

7. *Acceptance:* Accept your smallness.

8. *Cooperation:* Yield to others.

9. *Self-Control:* Keep a tight rein on the tongue.

10. *Silence:* Avoid empty speech.

11. *Gentleness:* Speak gently, truthfully, and simply.

12. *Humility:* Live a life of humility.

Chapter Two

ACTIVITIES FOR FAMILY SPIRITUALITY

In the presence of the angels I will sing to you.

— Psalm 138:1

Let us consider, then, how we ought to behave in the presence of God and his angels, and let us stand to sing the psalms in such a way that our minds are in harmony with our voices.

— THE RULE OF ST. BENEDICT, chap. 19

Every year in our local congregation, the children of the church present a Christmas pageant. No matter how many times I see this production, I never tire of seeing our youngest children dressed as angels, singing "Joy to the world the Lord has come."

A few years ago, the camel stole the show. We had painted only one side of the cardboard camel and it turned out to be the wrong side. When the camel trainer came in through a side door, he realized the problem. Rather than turn the camel around to face the correct direction and expose the duct tape and refrigerator company logo, the young man handling the cardboard camel, with an embarrassed grin, simply walked the camel backward into Bethlehem. It brought the house down.

Our family spiritual life will sometimes require us to "walk backward," to return to old traditional ways. If we are to sing with the angels, we must become like children and experience afresh the joy of God's presence in our home and family life. Benedict calls this activity the *Opus Dei,* the work of God. Indeed, without God actively at work in our family life, our prayers, devotions, and attempts at worship are like cardboard cutouts.

The activities in this chapter are designed to teach families how to *behave in the presence of God and his angels.* More than just how to behave, though, I hope these activities will begin to transform your family life into a daily sanctuary of worship, prayer, and devotion. God has intended our families to be a place of holy delight, a living pageant of God's joyful presence.

✝ Activity 8: Devotion Time

I'll be the first to admit that I am not a morning person. I don't bounce out of bed. I resist getting up before 8:00 A.M. My mind doesn't wake up until about noon and my most productive thinking hours of the day are between 10:00 P.M. and midnight.

By God's grace, I was given three natural alarm clocks: children. Over the past two decades my calling as a parent has forced me to get up and get our children up and into their day. Our morning family devotions are haphazard, with occasional readings of a devotional book on the way out the door while one son is trying to find shoes and the other is waiting for toast to pop up. None of us are morning people. Still, very few days go by without some practice of the spiritual disciplines we know will nurture our faith in God and grow us up in love. Once a week now, I invite a few neighbor teens over to join my teenage sons and me for 7:00 A.M. breakfast and devotions.

For a good devotional time with God, only two elements are needed: a set time for this spiritual discipline and a willingness to grow spiritually together in your life and faith in God. Benedict gives us an outline for devotions in chapter 9 of the Rule:

> *The following order is observed: Psalm 3 with doxology; Psalm 9 with a refrain, or at least chanted; an Ambrosian hymn; then six psalms with refrain. After the psalmody, a versicle is said and the prioress or abbot gives a blessing. When all are seated on the benches, the members in turn read three selections from the book . . . the inspired books of the Old and New Testaments.*
>
> (RB, 9)

Three Parts of a Devotional Time

1. **Pray the psalms:** The 150 psalms are given to us by God to teach us to pray together. Throughout the history of the Hebrew people and the Christian church, the psalms have been the centerpiece of our common worship. How are we to pray the psalms? Try this:

   ✤ Use a modern translation such as the New King James Version, the New International Version, or the New Revised Standard Version.

   ✤ Read one psalm out loud.

   ✤ Reflect upon one verse from this psalm.

2. **Sing songs of praise to God:** In one of the delightful stories from the early church (found in Acts 16) Paul and Silas,

chained up in jail for their faith, are singing songs of praise at midnight. Right in the middle of their songs, an earthquake shakes up the place, setting Paul and Silas free. Praise singing invokes the power of God to set us free from bondage.

✣ After the psalm, sing a song of praise.

✣ If your family doesn't know too many songs of praise, ask your pastor or priest for suggestions of resources for family praise singing: a hymnal, a praise songbook, a collection of favorite songs of faith. Or make up your own songs of praise.

3. **Read God's Word together:**

✣ Keep a Bible in the place where you have your time of devotion.

✣ If you have younger children who are beginner readers, use one of the special editions of the Bible available for these ages. There are a variety of family Bible devotional books and editions available. We've used the following in family devotions through the years: a *One Minute Bible* with 365 readings, children's Bible stories, *Closer Walk New Testament* with 365 readings from the New Testament, and *Daily Watchwords,* a daily devotional with short Scripture readings from the Old and New Testaments with verses of hymns included.

✣ Place a special bookmark to mark the place where you are reading.

✣ To begin, read through the Gospels: Matthew, Mark, Luke, and John.

✣ Following Benedict's guidance, offer your family a "blessing" at the end of your devotion time. Here are a few
possibilities:

"May God bless us all this new day."

"May God be gracious to us and bless us."
(Psalm 67:1)

"The Lord bless you and keep you, the Lord make
his face to shine upon you." (Numbers 6:24–25)

"May the peace of Christ be with you."

The name "Benedict" means "good words" or "blessings." Benedict offers parents a great way to start our day with our children:
with the prayers of the psalms, a song of praise to God, Scripture
read aloud, and a blessing spoken by a parent to the children.

✣ Activity 9: Make a Prayer Calendar

One of my favorite crafts from our children's elementary education is the homemade calendar. They all made them. We haven't
gotten rid of these treasures, though they are years out of date.
They are piled up in a school project box in our storage area, like
gold bullion in our bank vault of childhood memories.

A family prayer calendar can offer much richness to a family's
spiritual life. Benedict offers us guidance for praying through the
year, encouraging a seasonal approach to prayer together. In the
summer, he allows monks more sleep and shorter devotional times
to make up for the increased manual labor in the fields. In the
winter, he increases the length of time for reading.

We too celebrate the seasons of the year and the seasons of grace through the church calendar. One creative way to do this as a family is to make a family prayer calendar.

Materials

colored poster board

colored construction paper (twelve sheets)

old magazines

scissors

glue-stick

a spiral-bound month-at-a-glance calendar for the year ahead

colored pencils, crayons, or markers

How to Make a Family Prayer Calendar

✤ Assign months of the year to different family members.

✤ Cut out pictures, words, and images from magazines that represent each month and glue them onto the colored construction paper into a collage.

✤ Make a "frame" in the top half of the poster board to hold one of these monthly collages; attach triangles at corners so you can slip each corner of the collage into these holders.

✤ Write out prayers in the boxes of the "month-at-a-glance" calendar. Include prayers from the Bible, phrases from the psalms, prayers you find in prayer books, or devotional book prayers. Or write your own prayers. You don't need to have a prayer written into every day of the whole year. But try for at least one per week. Choose prayers that are fitting for the season: for example, "We give thanks to you, O Lord, we give thanks" (Psalm 75:1) for the third week of November.

✤ Slide the "Month-at-a-glance" prayer calendar into a slot in the bottom half of the poster board so that the appropriate month is showing and it can be slid out and changed monthly.

✤ Display your prayer calendar in a prominent place in your home.

✤ Change the calendar every month, putting in the new collage and turning over the prayers.

✤ Activity 10: Idea Bag for Sunday Worship

Sunday is a day to celebrate! We gather together to enjoy time with God, our Creator, our Savior, and our Restorer. Through worship each week, we personally are recreated by God, rescued from some of the destructive forces of the world and restored to newness of life, ready to reenter the everyday Monday-through-Saturday world once again. Benedict devoted two of his seventy-three brief chapters in the Rule to Sunday worship: when monks should rise, what order of service to follow, which Scripture passages to sing, what holy acts and words to offer to God. He even offers advice on what to do when members of the community *happen to arise too late*, an event most parents can relate to on Sunday morning.

What can make Sunday morning more enjoyable for the whole family? As a pastor, I've been very careful to build creative and enjoyable memories around Sunday worship, not forcing children to be "little adults," but offering them the opportunity to "come and see" where Jesus hangs out, to hear God's Word and see first hand God's people at worship. A friend sent me the following letter recently describing the medical value of regular worship with a community of faith.

Dr. Harold Koenig, M.D., associate professor of psychiatry and assistant professor of internal medicine at Duke University Medical School, has written a number of articles and a couple books on the subject of the effect of religion on health. I think you would find his book *Is Religion Good for Your Health* enjoyable and informative. Something that you might want to point out to your congregation is that the life expectancy for those who attend a church service at least once a week is seven years longer than those who rarely go to church. Anyway it appears that you are not only improving the quality, but also the quantity of life of those in your congregation.

Some would disagree, saying that Sunday worship is hazardous to your health. I knew a preacher's kids in Tennessee who were messing around in the first pew during their father's sermon. Mid-sentence, he stepped down from the pulpit, walked over, grabbed both boys by the hair, banged their heads together, and walked back up into the pulpit to continue his message, hardly missing a phrase.

That story came to me one Sunday morning while I was preaching at a church out in the countryside. Two of my sons, elementary school age at the time, had come with me that morning. Mom and the other son were home sick. During the sermon, I looked over to check on my boys. They were nowhere to be seen. Sudden panic was soon overcome by curiosity. As I continued preaching, I strolled down the center aisle and spotted them playing army commando under the pews on their bellies. They immediately saw the game was up, dove into their "Sunday worship bags," got out drawing journals, and sat still as I finished the final points of my message.

Sunday worship is tough on kids. We've always packed a Sunday worship bag for our young children, containing an assortment of items to keep children quiet and focus wandering minds and hands, while allowing adults to receive the fullest blessing of worshiping together with God's saints.

What to Pack in a Sunday Worship Bag

1. **Babies to toddlers:**

   a ziplock bag of cheerios

   a carton of juice

   picture books with quiet pages

   a puppet

   a favorite stuffed animal or blanket

   crayons and a scribble pad

2. **Preschool to primary:**

   fruit snacks

   picture books

   coloring books and crayons

   picture Bible with simple stories

3. **Primary to middle school:**

   children's Bible

   a reading book

journal with coloring pencils

faith workbooks with Scripture quizzes, puzzles, un-
scrambles, crosswords

mad-libs, fill in the pictures, and other quiet workbooks

✛ Activity 11: Learning the Lord's Prayer

There was a time when our children didn't speak a word of
English. A baby's first word is one of those holy, wonder-filled
moments in parenting. Speech is an acquired skill, learned over
years of intensive training. Now more than ever, in my forties, I
continue to deepen my language channels, seeking better ways to
move ideas up and down the river of language.

Prayer is no different. We learn to pray over years of intensive
training. We need to be taught to communicate with our heavenly Father. Jesus' first followers pleaded with him, "Lord, teach
us to pray!" The simple prayer he taught continues to offer us
instruction for a lifetime in the school of prayer. Try this exercise
as a way to learn to pray in your home.

Memorizing the Lord's Prayer

Commit the Lord's Prayer to memory as a family using the "seven-
day, seven-week" review method. Simply say one phrase per day
over seven days.

Sunday: Our Father, who art in heaven, hallowed be Thy
name.

Monday: Thy kingdom come, Thy will be done on earth as it
is in heaven.

Tuesday: Give us this day our daily bread.

Wednesday: Forgive us our debts (trespasses) as we forgive our debtors (those who trespass against us).

Thursday: Lead us not into temptation.

Friday: But deliver us from evil.

Saturday: For Thine is the kingdom and the power and the glory, forever, Amen. (KJV)

Try saying this phrase from the Lord's Prayer at the same time every day, for example, at dinner, just after the blessing, or at bedtime. Quiz children at other times of the day saying, "What is our prayer for the day?" Repeat this over seven weeks. After two months of daily repetition, the entire family will have this prayer tucked away for a lifetime of prayer instruction. Benedict encourages monks to recite this simple prayer twice a day, in the morning and in the evening:

> *Assuredly, the celebration of Lauds and Vespers must never pass*
> *by without the prioress or abbot reciting the entire Prayer of Jesus*
> *at the end for all to hear.* (RB, 13)

We recite this prayer out loud together sometimes as a bedtime prayer. Our children have known this prayer by heart since before they can remember. We keep welcoming our children back into the school of prayer. Through the Lord's Prayer Christ is teaching us the wonders and delights of learning to converse with our heavenly Father.

✤ Activity 12: Home for the Holidays

Ask any child, "What is your favorite day of the year?" The answer is not hard to guess: "Christmas!" My favorite memories of our family from my childhood are wrapped up in that gift box we call Christmas. Decorations, shopping trips, wish-lists, lights, baking cookies, festive music, friends and family members coming over, gifts piling up under the tree, surprises.

My mom used to tell us boys, when we were opening presents on Christmas Day, "Good things come in small packages." Among all the delightful childhood memories of Christmas, one of the best came in a small package: our celebration of Jesus' birth on Christmas Eve. We always attended a Christmas Eve service and sang "Silent Night" by candlelight. Later that night, my grandpa read the Christmas story aloud to his grandkids with only the candles and Christmas tree lights offering illumination. O holy night!

Benedict encourages families to celebrate *"the feasts of saints"* and *"all solemn festivals"* (RB, 14). Indeed, so important are the holy days of the year, that he organizes the life of his family of monks around the sacred calendar. Some parents who have not grown up in sacred traditions of the church are unfamiliar with the holy days of the church calendar.

Holy Days and Holidays

✤ **Advent Season:** the four weeks before Christmas Day; usually begins the last Sunday in November or the first Sunday in December.

✤ **Christmas Eve and Christmas Day:** December 24 and December 25; our celebration of Christ's birth.

✤ **Epiphany:** January 6, celebrating the Light of the World coming into our lives and the arrival of the "Wise Men," bringing kingly gifts of gold, frankincense, and myrrh.

✤ **Ash Wednesday:** the Wednesday six weeks before Easter Day, beginning the season of Lent.

✤ **Lent:** a six-week season in spring leading up to Holy Week and Easter, remembering the forty years of Israel in the wilderness and the forty days Christ spent in the wilderness fasting and being put to the test; "Lent" is an Old English word meaning "spring" or "season of renewal and growth."

✤ **Holy Week:** the week before Easter Day including **Palm Sunday, Maundy Thursday, and Good Friday**; we remember and celebrate the final week of Christ's life including his triumphal entry, the Last Supper, the Garden of Gethsemani, his arrest, trial, crucifixion, and burial.

✤ **Easter Day:** the great celebration of the Resurrection of Jesus Christ, God's victory over death, sin, and all evil; God's gift of eternal life to all.

✤ **Pentecost:** usually the last Sunday in May or the first Sunday in June; we celebrate the coming of the Holy Spirit as recorded in Acts 2.

✤ **Saints Days:** throughout the year special remembrance days celebrate the lives of the saints, our heroes of faith who have walked before us and offer us encouragement for our journey of faith. Some of the most popular saints' days include: St. Valentine (February 14), St. Patrick (March 17), St. Benedict (July 11), St. Francis (October 4), and All Saints (November 1).

Celebrating the Holy Days and Holidays as a Family

Every family enjoys family celebrations and annual traditions of one sort or another. Over the years, we've enjoyed adding new ideas we've gathered from others. These creative ideas, some drawn from church history, have added to the fun and richness of our family life together. I'll give an example here.

Every year we unpack our Nativity scene early in December. We have St. Francis of Assisi (1181–1226) to thank for the pleasure of the home Nativity scene. In 1223, Francis celebrated Christmas at Grecchio, Italy. There in Grecchio, Francis dramatized the birth of Christ with actual animals and actors at a hermitage just outside the village. The uneducated peasants of the village witnessed God's holy acts in living drama thanks to St. Francis's creativity. Nativity scenes in homes originate in St. Francis's practical way of celebrating Christ's birth.

Early in our family life, our friends Ben and Judy Herr told us about a custom of the "moving Nativity." Every year since, we reenact Christ's birth with a moving Nativity. We display only the stable and animals of our Nativity scene on the first Sunday of Advent. The shepherds and sheep are placed up high on a bookshelf, "on the hills around Bethlehem." Mary and Joseph are placed in another room. The Wise Men are placed in the room furthest from the stable.

One member of the family is placed in charge of moving Mary and Joseph daily. Another family member moves the Wise Men with their camels. Mary and Joseph arrive at the stable on Christmas Eve. Only then, on this holy night, does the Christ child appear in the manger, wrapped in linen cloth. The shepherds arrive on Christmas Day. The Wise Men continue to travel through the house after Christmas Day, arriving at the Nativity scene on

January 6, offering their gifts on Epiphany. Thus, the holy drama of Christ's birth comes alive throughout our home, with every family member involved, as we see the indescribable gift of God enacted before our eyes. For other ideas for family celebrations of holy days and holidays, look into these resources:

Gaither, Gloria, and Shirley Dobson. *Let's Make a Memory: Great Ideas for Building Family Traditions and Togetherness.* Dallas: Word, 1994.

Nelson, Gertrud Mueller. *To Dance with God: Family Ritual and Community Celebration.* New York: Paulist Press, 1986.

Robinson, Jo, and Jean Coppock Staeheli. *Unplug the Christmas Machine: How to Have the Christmas You've Always Wanted.* New York: Quill, 1991.

✤ Activity 13: The Glad Game

"Well, that's the game, you know, anyway."

"The — game?"

"Yes, the 'just being glad' game... the game was to just find something about everything to be glad about — no matter what 'twas," rejoined Pollyanna earnestly. "And we began right then — on the crutches."

"Well, goodness me! I can't see anythin' ter be glad about — gettin' a pair of crutches when you wanted a doll!"

Pollyanna clapped her hands.

"There is — there is," she crowed.... "Goosey! Why, just be glad because you don't — need — 'em!" exulted Pollyanna triumphantly. "You see it's just as easy — when you know how!"[6]

Benedict instructs his monks in the holy habit of praise and gladness. *Alleluia is always to be said with the psalms and the responsories* (RB, 15). One of the greatest dangers to the family according this wise guide is complaining and grumbling. The antidote to this disease is praise and gladness. The sacred word "Alleluia" expresses our glad hearts to God for the abundance of life, grace, and goodness offered to us through Jesus Christ.

A few years ago, we read *Pollyanna* aloud to our children at bedtime. We were delighted with Pollyanna's simple little game, "the glad game." Here's how you play.

How to Play the Glad Game

Begin on Monday morning at breakfast. Tell the whole family, "We're going to play a game this week called the Glad Game." Tell them the rules:

✛ Find something about everything to be glad about.

✛ Pick one of these glad tidings to share at dinner each night.

✛ At the dinner table have everyone say one thing they were glad about that day. We often ask our kids, "What was the best and the worst part of your day?"

✛ Challenge each other with the hard situations where there doesn't seem to be anything to be glad about, remembering Pollyanna's words: "You see, when you're hunting for the glad things, you sort of forget the other kind."

Encourage each other in the Glad Game, especially during tense situations in the family. Though we've never tried it, it might be fun at the end of the first week to present a prize (a sweet) to each member of the family for their glad hearts and rejoicing spirit. Try reading *Pollyanna* aloud together for bedtime stories to learn more about the Glad Game. We read this story to our children when they were preteens.

✚ Activity 14: Writing a Family Psalm

Scripture passages adorn the walls of our home. Some are cross-stitched, some glazed in ceramic, some written out by our children. The Hebrew people have practiced this art for thousands of years. Take a look at Deuteronomy, the sixth chapter.

> These commandments that I give you today are to be upon your hearts. Impress them on your children. Talk about them when you sit at home and when you walk along the road, when you lie down and when you get up. Tie them as symbols on your hands and bind them on your foreheads. Write them on the doorframes of your houses and on your gates. (Deuteronomy 6:6–9).

In our day, individualized faith and prayer has largely replaced structured family prayer. Contemporary forms of prayer have taken over more traditional forms. Spontaneous prayer is in vogue where once written prayers were offered. The pendulum of spiritual discipline and spiritual freedom keeps swinging. The following activity allows for creativity, spontaneity, and individual input, while creating a lasting, written family psalm.

Materials for Writing a Family Psalm

Bibles: if you have them use several translations or modern paraphrases paper: typing paper and colored construction paper

pens, colored pencils, or markers

picture frame: you can include a mat-frame if you like

How to Write a Family Psalm

✣ **Call the family together:** read Psalm 23 or 100 aloud and explain the activity.

✣ **Search the Psalms together:**

Using Bibles, spend fifteen minutes or more searching the psalms individually; everyone writes down five to ten phrases from various psalms.

Instruct family members to write down those phrases which speak to you about God, about your family, about faith, about what is most important for your family life.

Have an older sibling assist the younger children who are prereaders.

Play music and eat snacks while searching.

✣ **Listen to the psalms together:** take turns reading your selections aloud.

✣ **Compose your Family Psalm:**

Choose a "family scribe" to write down your Family Psalm.

Choose an opening phrase from one of the selections to begin your Family Psalm.

Phrase by phrase, write out your own Family Psalm together, allowing family members to offer suggestions of what to include.

Read your Family Psalm aloud together once you've finished composing it.

✛ **Display your Family Psalm:** place your Family Psalm in a picture frame and display it in a visible place in your home.

✛ Activity 15: Family Prayer Places

Travel around the world and you'll discover in millions of homes a place set apart for family spirituality. In some cultures this will simply be a candle and a bowl set on a side table. The candle is lit and the bowl is filled with an offering. Homes in other cultures have domestic shrines in memory of ancestors, with sacred objects and pictures of loved ones who have gone on before.

Such household places of worship and devotion are found in dirt-floored hovels as well as in marble-floored palaces, in high-rise apartments in crowded cities as well as in simple huts in rural areas. You will find highly educated religious people as well as unlearned common folk involved in daily acts of family spirituality.

Benedict set apart a special place in the monastic home for worship and prayer, the oratory:

> *The oratory ought to be what it is called, and nothing else is to be done or stored there. After the Opus Dei, all should leave in complete silence and with reverence for God, so that anyone who may wish to pray alone will not be disturbed by the insensitivity of another. Moreover, if at other times some choose to pray privately, they may simply go in and pray, not in a loud voice, but with tears and heartfelt devotion. (RB, 52)*

Not only does Benedict provide in the cloister for a place dedicated to prayer, he gives specific instruction for these private times of prayer in that place:

✚ Commit ourselves to prayer and don't allow other activities to crowd it out.

✚ Don't allow family members to disturb others who are praying.

✚ Pray in private.

✚ Pray from the heart, with reverence for God.

Though the family is quite different from the monastery, I still believe parents are wise to set aside certain places in the home where people can pray and not be disturbed, or at least be a little less disturbed. I love the prayer place I saw recently in our friend's home, where their sixth-grade daughter transformed a bedroom closet into a prayer closet complete with a flashlight, a pillow, a Bible, and a "Please Knock before Entering" sign.

How to Create Places for Family Prayer

✚ Collect ideas from family members about locations and items to be included in the Family Prayer Place.

✚ Offer guidance about what is needed for such a place: for example, a place that is away from distractions where a person is not as easily disturbed by others, a private place, a place that helps us focus on prayer, on God, on things of the heart.

✚ Offer suggestions for possible places: a walk-in closet, a corner of a bedroom, a spare room currently used for storage, a special chair in a quieter room of the house. One of the best places for kids is in their own bed.

✤ Collect items to be included in the Family Prayer Place: a candle; a Bible; devotional books; a kneeling bench; a cross or crucifix; a painting or piece of artwork that evokes beauty, prayer, holiness and God's presence; a tape or CD player with quiet instrumental music.

My Home Christ's Heart: An Essay on Family Spirituality

My first few years of full-time ministry as a youth pastor were a disaster. The youth group limped along with low attendance, bad attitudes, and worried parents. Several rough neighborhood kids kept showing up and upsetting the "good kids," including the senior pastor's daughter. I was delighted these street kids showed up. But they brought their foul language and body humor. Week after week, I felt frustrated with the terrible group dynamics and low morale among the youth. My boss, the senior pastor, began to question my leadership abilities.

After some time in personal crisis and prayer, I discerned Christ leading me to make a change: move the youth groups home. I started meeting in the afternoons with the rough boys in their blue-collar homes. We would sit around their messy bedrooms, listen to their music, and have "God-talk." They could ask any question about faith, God, heaven, hell, death, or life and expect an honest answer. Their friends dropped by and tuned into the conversations, hungry for spiritual truth. I met with the uptown social kids in the evenings in their homes, where we studied the Scriptures, prayed, and enjoyed informal time together. Once we stepped away from the church building and the official church youth program, I saw immediate signs of spiritual growth taking place in the lives of both groups of youth.

That early experiment in ministry revealed a lasting truth about spiritual growth: God designed us to grow spiritually, and we grow best in the place where we live, at home. Where does discipleship happen most effectively? Mark 1:29–31 reveals the Lord's plan for family spirituality:

> As soon as they left the synagogue, they went with James and John to the home of Simon and Andrew. Simon's mother-in-law was in bed with a fever, and they told Jesus about her. So he went to her, took her hand and helped her up. The fever left her and she began to wait on them.

Our faith in Christ grows best at home. We mature spiritually through daily disciplines of grace practiced in the home. We deepen our lives in Christ in our homes, in the daily domestic rhythm of life. Home is the place where we are healed, strengthened, taught to serve and love. Christ is our Teacher. The home is our school.

Family spirituality involves living with Christ at home, carrying out daily habits of godliness, serving, caring for others. Our Lord loves to come home with us, enter our daily lives, touch us at home. Jesus' first ministry center was in a home, the home of Simon and Andrew, with a few people, face to face, enjoying daily life together, eating, talking, and praying.

After his Ascension, the early church continued to meet regularly in homes for worship, prayer, study, fellowship, and service to the needy in the community. It was not until the fourth century that churches began to build church buildings and form ministry centers away from the home. One of the most encouraging movements of the Holy Spirit in our day is the movement back into the home with the development of home groups, cell groups, gatherings of believers in homes for what I like to call domestic discipleship.

Robert Munger wrote the modern faith parable "My Heart Christ's Home" to describe the important first steps into life with Christ. The sequel, describing ongoing spiritual growth through daily life in the home, could be called "My Home Christ's Heart." When we welcome Jesus into our heart, we give him Lordship over our homes and over our daily lives where we live. Here are a few ways we've found helpful to celebrate Christ's presence and practice family spirituality in our home:

✤ **Celebrate a "House Blessing."** Ask your pastor, your family, and a few members of your church to join you for a house blessing celebration. Even if you've lived in your home for years, if you've never dedicated your home to the Lord, set aside time for such a celebration. We've dedicated every home we've ever moved into to the Lord, praying through the entire home, welcoming Christ's presence into the house, declaring our home to be Christ's home. In twenty years of marriage, we've lived in seven homes, including six rentals. Each home has been a source of Christ's abundant blessing.

✤ **Mark your home with signs of faith.** The cross, candles, faith artwork, and Scripture verses adorn the walls and rooms of our home. The Jewish people were commanded by God to place Scripture verses in the doorways of their homes to remind them of God's faithfulness and steadfast love. I love to see signs of faith in people's homes when I come to visit. Our homes are personal expressions of our life in Christ. Signs of faith in our home also offer us God's gift of protection. Because of the Passover sign on their doorways, the Hebrew children were protected from death (see Exodus 12). Jesus offers us protection from evil, from bad spirits and spiritual ills. He taught us to pray, "Deliver us from evil." Especially at night, we pray with our children, asking the Lord to protect us and bless us while we sleep. We recite the night blessing from Psalm 4:8, "I will lie down and sleep in peace, for you alone, O Lord, make me dwell in safety."

✤ **Live daily with Christ in your home life.** Family spirituality occurs in the ordinary events of our lives. Benedict declared this mundane approach to the spiritual life when he called monks to *regard all utensils and goods of the monastery as sacred vessels of the altar, aware that nothing is to be neglected* (RB, 31). As an undergraduate student, I worked in a sorority house as a houseboy. Every Sunday I mopped the floors in the kitchen along with a list of other chores. No one checked up on my job and I often did the bare minimum. One Sunday evening, I was fasting and meditating while mopping the floor in a sloppy way. It was as though I heard an inner voice asking me, "Who are you working for?" Convicted of my sloppy work and my sloppy attitude toward Christ, I offered a prayer of commitment, "Lord, I'll try to do my work for you, not for the sorority house and not for money." I was beginning to learn the lesson of family spirituality as expressed in Paul's instructions: "Whatever you do, work at it with all your heart, as working for the Lord, not for people, since you know that you will receive an inheritance from the Lord as a reward. It is the Lord Christ you are serving" (Colossians 3:23–24).

✤ **Offer hospitality in the name of Christ.** The task of hospitality, including meal preparations and caring for people when they come into our homes, shapes our hearts into the image of Jesus. The kingdom of God is filled with "No Name, No Fame" servants. God loves to honor behind-the-scenes heroes, people who never get recognized for their greatness because they are quiet, ordinary people doing everyday domestic tasks, serving others in Jesus' name. When Jesus healed Simon Peter's mother-in-law, she immediately began to serve the people who had come into her home. Serving others means caring for the needs of others, helping others live well through offering hospitality to people in our homes. This is truly following Christ. Family spirituality unfolds through simple acts of hospitality.

✤ **Pray blessings for others:** Family spirituality means telling Jesus about people in our lives (neighbors, family members, friends, others) who need help, blessings, healing. Like Simon, who told Jesus of his ailing mother-in-law, we also bring people to Jesus so that he can heal them, give them help. In our local congregation, we have teams of intercessors, "Houses of Prayer," organized in neighborhoods, praying Christ's blessings to come to neighbors. We pray five blessings for our neighbors using the BLESS outline:

  B Body (physical needs and healing)

  L Labor (work, employment, adequate income)

  E Emotions (heart and soul blessings)

  S Social (relationships among family and friends)

  S Spiritual (salvation, spiritual growth through prayer, Bible study, worship, and service).

Chapter Three

ACTIVITIES FOR FAMILY DISCIPLINE

Train a child in the way he should go, and when he is old he will not turn from it. —Proverbs 22:6

The abbot and prioress must exercise the utmost care and concern for the wayward because, "it is not the healthy who need a physician, but the sick" (Matthew 9:12). Therefore they ought to use every skill of a wise physician.

— The Rule of St. Benedict, chap. 27

Come with me to Hobb's Cabin. A log-cabin built back in the mid-1800s by pioneers, Hobb's Cabin is located on top of limestone bluffs overlooking the Savage Gulf wilderness area of central Tennessee. Mr. Hobb built his cabin just steps away from a natural spring, bubbling forth at the top of that hillside.

Back in the late 1980s I hiked the nine miles with a friend and my black Labrador, arriving at Hobb's Cabin at sundown on a muggy August day. The three of us drained several two-liter water bottles, as no water source presented itself the entire nine miles along the dry river bed trail. One of our first tasks upon arrival was to refill the water bottles at the spring.

The spring was clogged up with summer debris and covered over with a thin film of algae. We set to work clearing away the leaves, sticks, and trash from other hikers. We had to wait until the morning before the spring freshened up and we could dip our thirsty mouths into the cool spring water and refill our water bottles for the return hike home.

Discipline doesn't feel good nor is it a favorite form of entertainment. In our modern Western world, pleasure and leisure motivate many of the life choices we make. This can spell disaster within the family. Much of parenting requires discipline: first, the discipline of clearing away the debris which keeps our children from bubbling forth with God's goodness and grace; second, the discipline of waiting, trusting God to bring forth eternal life within our children when we've done what we can do. These two forms of discipline, active and submissive, are found spread across the eight chapters on discipline in the Rule of St. Benedict.

The word "discipline," commonly thought to mean "punishment," actually has its roots in the word for education, training, or instruction. Discipline at its heart is training: placing ourselves in God's training and offering God's holy training to our children. When we follow the wise guidance of Scripture and train up our children in the way they should go, we will discover their lives springing forth with God's living water of eternal life and love. The activities in this chapter illustrate a few ways to clear away some of the clutter from the divine springs in our family life and watch God's wonderful life bubble forth.

✠ Activity 16: The Bedtime Train

About ten years ago, we boarded Amtrak as a family and rode three days across the country. Each time we switched trains or got off for a stop, our preschool child broke into tears, worried that we would miss the train. We developed a set of rituals for counting heads and pieces of luggage as well as getting to the platform with plenty of time before departure to allay our son's fears. After visiting friends in Minneapolis, we boarded the train at midnight. After we found our seats, we went through our normal head count, baggage count, and nighttime rituals to help settle our children for the night journey across the great northern prairie in peace.

Bedtime rituals accomplish this same result, offering parents and children a set structure or discipline for ending the day together. Whenever I've been in a home without such discipline, I find myself becoming anxious and unsettled. Not only do I want the house to get quiet so that I can enjoy uninterrupted conversation with adults, but I see children who obviously are spinning out of control without the supporting structure of bedtime rituals.

Trying to raise children without such daily disciplines as a set bedtime routine is like trying to drive a train without tracks. The day ends as a wreck. Parents are irritable and crabby. Children crash into beds overtired and undernurtured. Here then are some ideas for boarding the Bedtime Train.

✠ With children age five and up, agree together on "Bed" Time and on "Getting Ready for Bed" Time. Parents have authority given by God to set times for children and maintain these times, but there is a great value in working with children to make decisions concerning their lives. We alter bedtimes according to the age of each child, the night of the week (school night or nonschool night), and the time of the year (summer or winter).

✤ If possible, provide separate beds for each child. Benedict offered this same practical wisdom fifteen hundred years ago, *"Members are to sleep in separate beds"* (RB, 22).

✤ Develop a routine for boarding the Bedtime Train:

1. **All Aboard!:** Let family members know it's time for getting ready for bed.

2. **Bathroom Time:** Move children to bathrooms for personal care of hygiene: bathing, brushing teeth, getting a drink of water, using the toilet.

3. **Pajamas:** Change into bedclothes.

4. **Hugs and Kisses:** Say goodnight to family with kisses and hugs.

5. **Storytime:** Meet together in one bedroom for story time. Choose appropriate age-level books to read aloud to your children. Over the years, we've read over a hundred great novels (more than 250 pages each) and thousands of children's stories aloud to our children. In the last two months, we've read Madeleine L'Engle's *A Swiftly Tilting Planet*, Margaret Craven's *I Heard the Owl Call My Name*, and Isak Dinesen's short novel *Babette's Feast*. My wife and I alternate reading books. When choosing books, we turn to such resources as William Kilpatrick's *Books That Build Character: A Guide to Teaching Your Child Moral Values through Stories*.[7] Kilpatrick offers an excellent book list in a variety of categories for different ages with brief descriptions. We like to read for fifteen to

thirty minutes together. Include in your regular reading diet stories from the Bible.

6. **Prayertime:** Offer up simple nighttime prayers, speaking directly to God and teaching your children, through your example, how to pray conversational prayers to God. Offer thanks for the day, ask for forgiveness for things done wrong, ask God for protection, and tell God, "I love you."

7. **Blessing:** Pronounce a nighttime blessing together. We have learned several of these sentences of blessings from the Psalms. Our favorite is one used by monks every night at Compline.

> In peace will I both lie down and sleep, for you alone, O LORD, make me to dwell in safety.
>
> (Psalm 4:8)

With these nighttime rituals, our children are all aboard for another adventure across the mountains and prairies of Dreamland.

✚ Activity 17: Truth or Consequences

On a recent six-hour road trip, with our family of five in the car, a radiator hose burst. I kept ignoring the sight of steam escaping from the car, thinking it was from someone else's car. We were having too much fun with a family travel game, and I wasn't about to be interrupted.

At last, after an hour of freeway driving, my son said, "Dad, I think our car is smoking." We all turned and saw what I had been seeing for an hour. I had to face the truth: something is wrong with this car. I also had to face the consequences: if I didn't pull over and fix a broken radiator hose, the car would force me to pull over to replace an overheated engine block.

By God's grace, we pulled into a gas station that was still open at 7:30 at night. The mechanic, Salaam, was able to get the repair done quickly and we were on the road in less than an hour. "Salaam" is Arabic for "peace." This mechanic lived out his name that night by bringing peace of mind to a family on a long road trip.

Loving discipline in the family often means facing the truth of a problem, refusing to avoid the unpleasant consequences, getting the "car" repaired, and then proceeding along our way in peace. You might call this approach to discipline "Truth or Consequences." When you are faced with a problem in the family requiring discipline, try playing Truth or Consequences.

✚ A parent plays "Bob," the game show host.

✚ Bob chooses an offending family member to step up and "play the game."

✚ Bob asks the contestant to choose a category: truth or consequences.

✚ **Truth:** the "studio audience," all the family members involved, are allowed to ask the contestant one question relating to the family problem. The contestant is required to offer "truth," an honest answer, to each question. Bob is then allowed to offer "truth," or an honest reply, to the family member requiring discipline.

✚ **Consequences:** each family member chooses one activity, discipline, or task for the family member to perform. A parent acts as judge to select the appropriate "consequence" for the out-of-line family member. As Benedict wisely counsels, *There*

> *ought to be due proportion between the seriousness of a fault and*
> *the measure . . . of discipline* (RB, 24).

If a child refuses to "play the game" of Truth of Consequences, that child simply adds to his troubles and increases the seriousness of the fault, thus increasing the seriousness of the consequence. This leads a parent to more intensive forms of discipline.

✠ Activity 18: Make Your Own Hockey "Time-Out" Box

Every year in our village, our grade school sponsors a Halloween carnival. One of the activities kids enjoy most is locking up adults in the Hockey Penalty Box. You don't get out until some other adult or child has mercy on you and buys more tickets.

There comes a time in every family, like in every hockey game, when a player commits a penalty and needs to spend time in the penalty box. Benedictine monasteries employ such a form of discipline:

> *Those guilty of a serious fault are to be excluded from both the*
> *table and the oratory. No one in the community should associate*
> *or converse with them at all.* (RB, 25)

✠ Choose a place in the house as the location for your Time-Out Box. This place should be easily viewable by parents, yet free from distractions and diversions for children. The simplest Time-Out Box is a chair placed in a location that can be easily monitored by a parent. Remove temptations (remote control to the TV, music, books, comics, and toys) that might distract that "hockey player" from getting back "onto the ice."

✤ Decide on the appropriate time-out period. To begin with, try one minute per year: a five-year-old spends five minutes in Time-Out. Increase the time with the seriousness of the fault.

✤ Give the child a clear notice that the timer has begun. For example: "You hit your brother. That foul places you in the Time-Out Box for fifteen minutes. I will come get you at the end of the time and then you can go play again."

✤ If your child chooses to go back "out onto the ice" before the time is up, send him or her back to the Time-Out Box with a warning and add time to the penalty.

✤ For some more serious fouls, the time in the box may include missing important family events such as dinner together, family game time, television, or an outing.

✤ For teenage children, the Time-Out Box might include withheld privileges: no access to the family car, staying home rather than spending time at a friend's house, or missing a school sporting event.

✤ At the end of the discipline time, have "a coach-to-player" talk about the rules of the game and fair play, and then send your child back "out onto the ice."

✤ Activity 19: Creative Corrections and Positive Discipline

I attended a weekend seminar a few years ago on restorative justice. The presenters opened a whole new vision of justice to my eyes regarding our criminal justice system. Most of our present system is based upon punitive justice: punishing offenders for breaking the law. Restorative justice goes a few steps further: seeking to restore offenders back to the human community. Many stories of creative programs of restorative justice were told. Meanwhile, our nation continues to build new prisons and struggles with how to treat those who have violated the law. (*The Family Cloister*, 93)

How can we as parents offer our children restorative justice? What are the methods for offering our children positive, loving discipline? When discipline is viewed as merely "punishing offenders for breaking the law," parental discipline will not be very effective in building lasting character in our children. When we view discipline from a Benedictine perspective, this aspect of parenting becomes like athletic training or like taking medicine. Discipline is simply one more method for building people up in faith, hope, and love.

Of course, children are not so quick to see discipline as positive or creative or helpful. Most children, at least some of the time, will bump against the guardrails, test the line, tear down the walls, disrespect authority, and resent any attempts to limit their freedom. Of this we can be certain. Children do not like to be disciplined. Listen to what Scripture tells us:

Our fathers disciplined us for a little while as they thought best; but God disciplines us for our good, that we may share in his holiness. No discipline seems pleasant at the time, but painful. Later on, however, it produces a harvest of righteousness and peace for those who have been trained by it.
(Hebrews 12:9–11)

Creative Corrections: Benedictine Steps of Discipline

The following steps of discipline are drawn from the Rule, chapter 28.

1. **Verbal Discipline:**

   ✤ *The ointment of encouragement:* We are wise to pay attention to this insight of Benedict, that encouragement is a form of discipline, or training in righteousness.

   ✤ *Frequent reproof for faults:* This form of discipline can easily become nagging, especially when the child knows mom and dad don't really mean what they say and when there are no consequences for repeated faults. Nonetheless, the Bible calls us as parents to offer our children consistent verbal correction for faults (see Proverbs 3:11, 12; 29:15).

2. **Spiritual Discipline:**

   ✤ *The medicine of divine Scripture:* the Bible describes itself as "living and active, sharper than any double-edged sword, penetrating even to dividing soul and spirit . . . judging the thoughts and attitudes of the heart" (Hebrews 4:12). We are wise to employ such an effective tool of discipline by regularly bringing Scripture into our training sessions: speaking Scripture to our children, having our children read Scripture, study Scripture, memorize Bible verses and meditate upon certain sentences or phrases from the Bible.

   ✤ *All the members should pray for them so that God, who can do all things, may bring about the health of the sick one:* We have a "great high priest, Jesus the Son of God," who is able to "sympathize with our weaknesses." Through prayer we approach God's "throne of grace with confidence, so that we may receive mercy and find grace to help us in our time of need" (Hebrews 4:14–16).

3. **Physical Discipline:**

✠ *Applying the compresses:* Benedict refers to limiting a person's privileges or putting a squeeze on a family member's freedom. This form of discipline is especially powerful in the teenage years, when personal freedoms are so highly valued and the price tag of responsibility so easily disregarded.

✠ *The cauterizing iron of excommunication:* This is what we call "Time-Out," or removal from the family circle and isolation for a set amount of time.

✠ *Strokes of the rod:* discipline of the body when employed with love (not in the heat of anger) is clearly spoken of in Scripture and in the Rule as another means of loving discipline when other forms of discipline have failed.

✠ Activity 20: Player, Coach, and Referee – A Role Play

One of the most successful college basketball coaches of all time, Johnny Wooden of UCLA fame, committed himself early in his career to being a lifelong learner at the game of basketball. Every year, though he continued to pile up national championships (ten in twelve years) and undefeated seasons (a total of four), he'd focus his attention on mastering another aspect of the game.

One year it was offensive rebounding, the next year, the pic and roll.

Parents are also lifelong learners. Once the kids grow up and begin raising children of their own, parents get to learn all over again how to be grandparents. Parenting is for beginners. Children are mysteries a lifetime will not completely unveil. There are no degrees, no certificates, little training for new parents, except the practical experience of raising children.[8] An enjoyable and practical way to learn together as a family is role-playing. I suggest trying a role-playing game called "Player-Coach-Referee."

✤ Set up three chairs in room: a "Player" chair, a "Coach" chair and a "Referee" chair.

✤ Get volunteers to play the Player, the Coach, and the Referee.

✤ Each threesome gets five minutes to act out, to improvise their role using the situations below.

✤ Choose a situation, depending upon the age of your children. Feel free to alter any of these to better suit your imagination and particular family issues.

    1. **The Locker Room Fight:** The Player has just gotten into a push-and-shove fight in the locker room after his team lost the game. The Coach broke up the fight and is trying to talk some sense into the Player. The Referee is also in the locker room and offers some words of wisdom to the Player, but the Coach keeps interrupting him.

    2. **Trouble on the Sidelines:** The Coach is yelling directions at kids on the court. He's getting out of control with his emotions and starts yelling at the Referee. The Player on the sidelines asks the Coach to settle down because he's embarrassing the team. The Coach tells the

Player to sit down and keep quiet; it's not his business. The Referee gives the Coach a technical foul for unsportsmanlike conduct. The Player steps in and defends his Coach before the Referee.

3. **The Forgotten Gear:** The Player has left his soccer cleats at home and has to tell the Coach. The Coach is unhappy, since he doesn't have enough kids to make up a full team without the Player. The Referee steps in to ask why the team hasn't taken the field to start the game. The Coach has to explain that his Player has forgotten his gear and that they don't have enough players. The Referee lectures the Player on responsibility.

4. **"I Never Get in the Game!":** The Player is upset on the sidelines of a basketball court because he's been sitting on the bench the whole game. He makes some pretty loud comments about "the coaching." The Coach overhears and comes down the bench to have a "little talk" with the Player. The Referee for this game happens to be the Player's dad (or mom). The Referee calls a Referee's time-out to talk over the situation with the Player and the Coach.

5. **Picking Dandelions in the Outfield:** The Coach is encouraging his players at a baseball game. His team is out in the field. The Player is way out in right field daydreaming, picking dandelions. The Coach yells directions to the Player. The Player can't quite hear what the Coach is saying. The Referee acts as a "relay" of the messages between the Coach and the Player. The Referee can put his or her own spin on this interaction.

6. **Saturday Soccer Mania:** The Player and the Coach are celebrating at a Saturday soccer game because they just won their first game of the season. They are replaying the highlights of the game, encouraging each other. The Referee politely at first asks them to get off the field since the next game is about to begin. They ignore the Referee. The Referee must get more and more direct and forceful to get them to move.

7. **The Ball Hog:** During a time-out at a basketball game, the Player complains to his Coach. The problem is the other shooting guard on the team. He's truly a ball hog. He won't pass the ball. Right now, the ball hog is over at the water-faucet, getting a drink. The Coach tries to explain to the Player how to handle ball hogs. The Referee calls the teams back onto the floor and also steps over to the Player to offer some advice about dealing with ball hogs. Mix it up a bit by making the Referee the ball hog's mom or dad.

✤ Activity 21: Seed Time

A single mom I know deals with her child's misbehavior through activities she calls "Seed Time." "I grew up gardening," she explained. "Through our 'seed time' together, my son is learning important life concepts which empower him to solve his problems."

Benedict offers a forgiving approach to discipline. Those who have been removed from active community life are received back again and again with the provision that *they must first promise to make full amends for leaving. Let them be received back, but as a test of humility they should be given last place. If they leave again, or even a third time, they should be readmitted under the same condition* (RB, 29).

Granted, Benedict is speaking of monks who leave the confines of the monastery. The walls and vows of a monastery offer stability to the individual and to the whole community. Those who break vows or go "over the wall" by leaving the monastery are welcomed back into the community, but with specific approaches to reintroduction. Similarly, those who break family rules and disregard the "walls" of family discipline are to be welcomed back, but with specific means for bringing them back into the fold. Benedict varies his approach to discipline depending upon the person, including personality type and age. *Every age and level of understanding should receive appropriate treatment* (RB, 30).

Here are a few activities for Seed Time. These are positive ways to support wavering children and welcoming them back into family life through positive discipline. A real key to this approach to positive discipline is being with your child and working together with him or her in sowing good seeds of a new activity. If you don't have time or patience to spend with a grumpy, misbehaving child, a different approach to discipline will be a better choice.

Ten Seed Time Activities

1. Take a walk outside together to observe growing things: plants, trees, flowers, a forest. Try collecting similar items on each of these walks: leaves, rocks, flowers, seeds.

2. Climb a tree together to sit still and listen to the wind.

3. Play catch with a baseball and mitts, or pass a soccer ball together.

4. Garden together: always keep some bulbs or seeds on hand for planting at various times of the year.

5. Pull weeds together in a flower bed.

6. Spread some mulch or a bag of topsoil as ground cover in flower beds.

7. Browse together a book of artwork or a color photo magazine like *National Geographic*.

8. Build something together: get out a Seed Time box of Legos, K'nex, Erector Set, or model. Work on building this project only during Seed Time.

9. Water all the plants in the house.

10. Bake cookies together, encouraging your child to do much of the measuring, mixing, shaping, and spatula work.

✤ Activity 22: The Mending Wall

> Before I built a wall I'd ask to know
> What I was walling in or walling out,
> And to whom I was like to give offense.
> — ROBERT FROST, from *Mending Wall*[9]

Discipline in the family is like building and mending walls. Discipline demands the best parents have to offer. Once the "walls" of discipline are built, they are tested and challenged and need mending. More importantly, those who have been disciplined or walled off through their violations of family rules need to be brought back into the fold. Benedict writes of this critical parenting task:

> It is the responsibility of the abbot or prioress to have great concern and to act with all speed, discernment, and diligence in order not to lose any of the sheep entrusted to them. They should realize that they have undertaken care of the sick, not tyranny over the healthy. (RB, 27)

Like Robert Frost and his neighbor, "meet to walk the line and set the wall between us once again." Using Benedict as our guide, I invite you to "walk the line" of your parental disciplinary "walls," reviewing how you've been disciplining your children and mending any of these "walls" with wisdom from Scripture and from the Rule (RB, 27).

Parenting Discipline Inventory: Mending Walls

Evaluate your parental discipline using the Benedictine principles of discipline below, drawn from the Rule, chapter 27. Assess your approach to discipline in light of each statement below, with (a) strongly agree; (b) agree; (c) disagree, (d) strongly disagree.

1. A parent *must exercise the utmost care and concern for the wayward because, "it is not the healthy who need a physician, but the sick"* (Matthew 9:12).

2. A parent *ought to use every skill of a wise physician. Support the wavering sisters or brothers, urge them to be humble as a way of making satisfaction.*

3. After disciplining their children, parents should *console them lest they be overwhelmed by excessive sorrow* (2 Corinthians 2:7).

4. Discipline is an expression of a parent's love, *as the apostle also says, "Let love be reaffirmed"* (2 Corinthians 2:8).

5. Parents are wise to *pray for the one* being disciplined.

6. It is the parents' responsibility *to have great concern and to act with all speed, discernment, and diligence in order not to lose any of the sheep entrusted to them.*

7. Parents should realize *that they have undertaken care of the sick, not tyranny over the healthy.*

8. Parents are called by God to build up the weak and offer themselves in service to their children as a shepherd takes care of the flock. As the Scriptures warn, "Should not the shepherds take care of the flock?" Like a shepherd, a parent's calling is to *strengthen the weak ... heal the sick ... bind up the injured ... bring back the strays ... search for the lost* (Ezekiel 34:2–4).

9. Parents are wise to *imitate the loving example of Christ, the Good Shepherd, who left the ninety-nine sheep in the mountains and went in search for the one sheep that had strayed.* This does not mean we neglect our well-behaved children. Rather, it means we try to imitate Christ, the Good Shepherd, in our relationship with children when they stray.

10. Parents offer children Christ's compassion through discipline and need to take great care to restore children fully after a time of discipline. *So great was Christ's compassion for its weakness that "he mercifully placed it on his sacred shoulders" and so carried it back to the flock* (Luke 15:5).

Chapter Four

ACTIVITIES FOR FAMILY HEALTH

Long life to you! Good health to you and your household!
And good health to all that is yours!   —1 Samuel 25:6

We brought nothing into the world, and we can take nothing
out of it. But if we have food and clothing, we will be content
with that.   —1 Timothy 6:7–8

*So regulate and arrange all matters that souls may be saved
and the members may go about their activities without justifiable
grumbling.*   — THE RULE OF ST. BENEDICT, chap. 41

One of our first dates before we were married was baking bread.
We mixed and kneaded the dough, and then waited for the dough
to rise. We formed the loaves, put them in to bake, and then
waited. Each of these activities led us to the best part of the
evening together: the taste of hot bread fresh out of the oven.
That was a date hard to match!

Bread is basic to family life. All families must eat. Jesus taught us a simple and practical prayer: "Give us this day our daily bread." The activities in chapter 4 concern the health of the family: the physical health as well as the spiritual well-being of the family. Benedict places a priority on the spiritual life, making arrangements in the monastery for the nourishment of souls, but not at the expense of the physical life, the feeding of bodies. He offers ten chapters on such ordinary topics as kitchen help, menus, what to drink, when to eat, and caring for people when their bodies get sick.

Whenever I retreat to a Benedictine monastery, my spirit is free to grow because my bodily needs are well cared for. Monastic retreat rooms are simple but comfortable. Monastic food is mostly vegetarian, but flavorful. Monastic spirituality honors the body while pointing to the spirit, the core of our life in God. The eight activities below deal with bodily needs while planting us deeper into the rich soil of the spirit.

✟ Activity 23: Planting a Victory Garden

The government helped families stay healthy during lean war years by promoting Victory Gardens, small plots where families grew vegetables. The size of the garden is not important. Think small. When our children were toddlers, we began with a ten foot square garden in a borrowed corner of a friend's backyard. Some other ideas for a Victory Garden include a planter box on a sunny back porch, a window ledge garden, or a flower pot garden.

Benedict helped his monastic family stay healthy by providing monks with a "Cellarer," the person in charge of the kitchen, the menu, the food, and the garden. Every monastery I've visited has a garden to provide food for the community. We also took up gardening early in our parenting years: partially because we love fresh, home-grown fruits, herbs, flowers, and vegetables on our table. But we've also learned some of God's best lessons together as a family through this practical classroom, through planting a Victory Garden.

We are not expert gardeners and have made lots of mistakes over the years. Like much in life, gardening is learned by trial and error. Here are some ideas that may be of help in starting a family tradition of a Victory Garden.

Planning your Victory Garden

✤ Begin in the New Year, making a family plan to "plant a Victory Garden."

✤ Discuss together what types of things you would like to grow as a family.

✤ Plan where your garden will be planted and even lay out a garden design.

Preparing the Soil

✤ Rent or borrow a Rotor-tiller.

✤ Remove rocks and roots from the soil.

✤ Add your own family compost to your garden soil. Look in your local library or other resources about building your own compost bin.

✤ Ask locals about soil conditions and natural additives for soil improvements.

Collecting What You Need

✤ Go shopping with your children, making it a Victory Garden expedition.

✤ Buy seeds, seedlings, natural fertilizers, soil helpers, and anti-pest aids.

✤ Gather together all your gardening tools, buckets, gloves and other items in one place in a shed or garage.

Planting Seeds and Starts

✤ Lay out the Victory Garden into plots or rows for various types of plants, vegetables, and flowers.

✤ Help your children plant seeds and seedlings in the soil, using a hands-on approach to discovering the wonder of seeds, roots, soil, and God's creation.

Caring for the Garden

✤ Water your Victory Garden regularly.

✤ Weed the garden with your children.

✤ Thin out and tie up plants as needed.

✤ Try natural approaches to bug control. We had neighbors who turned loose thousands of ladybugs in their Victory Garden to counteract an aphid attack.

Harvesting

At last comes the day you've awaited for months: your first harvest!

✢ Out at your Victory Garden, celebrate your first harvest by offering a prayer of thanks to God for his goodness and for this good earth filled with growing things. Sing an appropriate song or hymn, such as "For the Beauty of the Earth."

✢ Continue to harvest and to give away your harvest until the final plants produce their last fruit, flower, or vegetable.

✢ When October rolls around, it is time to prepare the garden for the winter, giving thanks to God for all the wonderful gifts and lessons you've learned from your Victory Garden.

I like what Marjorie Waters, a gardener-mom, writes about hands-on learning through gardening. "It's important that the kids see the garden as theirs rather than yours, that they have a good time, get their hands down in the earth, appreciate the wonder of watching plants grow and make flowers and food and know that they have a part in it all. In the complicated world our kids live in, these are real gifts."[10]

✢ Activity 24: The Kitchen Chore Chart

We've been playing the game of "Kitchen Clean-Up" with our children for eighteen years, and like most parents I know, we daily encourage our children to get their chores done. Some habits develop over a lifetime. Benedict assumed that all monks help out with kitchen tasks.

> *The members should serve one another. Consequently, no members will be excused from kitchen service unless they are sick or engaged in some important business of the monastery, for such service increases reward and fosters love.* (RB, 35)

We use two charts as a family to help us sort out who does what in the house and when these tasks get done. The first chart is a calendar with each week of the year labeled with a letter: A, B, C, D, through the year. The other chart is our Chore Chart. We rotate kitchen chores each week, according to what week it is, an "A" week, "B" week, "C" week, or "D" week. Here's a sample:

DAILY KITCHEN JOBS				
	COOK's HELPER	UNLOAD	LOAD	CLEAR/CLEAN
A	Thomas	Stefan	Jonathan	Dad
B	Dad	Thomas	Stefan	Jonathan
C	Jonathan	Dad	Thomas	Stefan
D	Stefan	Jonathan	Dad	Thomas

As parents, we refer to the chore calendar, see what week it is, and announce to the household the task at hand. For example, "Today is a 'C' week. The dishwasher needs to be loaded. Thomas, please come do your job."

Along with kitchen chores, we ask our children to participate in house clean-up daily and weekly. These tasks are chosen at a family meeting once or twice a year. Each household and age-level is different. Though we've tried, we haven't been very successful in matching chore responsibility to age level and ability. With family chores, we are definitely a work in progress.

We post these charts on our refrigerator and refer to them regularly to keep each other motivated and on track of what we've all agreed to do. Here's a sample of our daily and weekly chore charts. Now that our oldest son has gone off to college, we've had to cover for his chores.

Daily Chores

JONATHAN: Make bed, sweep wood floor

STEFAN: Make bed, take out trash

THOMAS: Make bed, care for Sofie (our black Labrador) with food, water, walk

Weekly Chores (Saturday)

JONATHAN: Wood floors, living room, dust and oil woodwork, clean bedroom

STEFAN: Shake rugs, sweep porch, Sofie bath, clean bedroom, recycle

THOMAS: Vacuum upper floor, wash car, clean bathroom, clean bedroom

✠ Activity 25: The Giveaway Game

The goods of the monastery, that is, its tools, clothing, or anything else, should be entrusted to members whom the prioress or abbot appoints and in whose manner of life the prioress or abbot has confidence. The abbot and prioress will, as they see fit, issue to them the various articles to be cared for and collected after use.

— THE RULE OF ST. BENEDICT, chap. 32

At a family meeting, tell everyone that the family will be playing the Giveaway Game at the next family meeting, and everyone needs to bring one item of their belongings to give away to some-one else. During the week, meet with each child and go through drawers and closets together to thin out belongings that can be given away. These may include clothes, shoes, games, books, toys, stuffed animals, blankets, bedding, or other possessions.

A few guidelines may help you and your children get into the giveaway spirit. Ask a few questions:

✝ What haven't I worn this past year?

✝ What doesn't fit anymore?

✝ Which toys have stayed on the toy shelf for too long?

✝ What in this room would make another little girl or boy happy to receive as a gift?

✝ Which things do I really need and which ones don't I need anymore?

I do not believe in forcing any child to give up a possession. As the preacher tells us in the Book of Ecclesiastes, "There is a time for everything . . . a time to keep and a time to throw away" (3:1, 6). If a child needs to "keep" an item, help that child find something to give away. At the next family meeting, have everyone bring their treasures as tokens for playing the Giveaway Game.

Playing the Giveaway Game

✝ Have the members of the family describe something they liked about one of their "giveaway" treasures.

✝ Ask God to bless the people who will receive these belongings.

✝ Place all the items in boxes, and deliver them to a local thrift store, Goodwill, Salvation Army, or other charitable organization that receives such donations.

Operation Christmas Child

One variation on this game is a project our family and church has participated in for the past few years called "Operation Christmas Child Box" with a world relief organization called Samaritan's Purse, under the direction of the Rev. Franklin Graham, son of the Rev. Billy Graham. Every October, we pack one shoe box per child with certain items listed in the organization's brochure. These items may include the following:

hygiene items: a tooth brush, tooth paste, soap, a wash cloth, a comb, fingernail clippers

small stuffed animals such as beanie babies

toys (but no war toys allowed)

candy (but no chocolate or candy that will melt)

small coloring books and crayons

pencils, color markers, child scissors, and other craft items

One Sunday is devoted to packing the boxes and taking up an offering for shipping costs. The following Sunday, we have the children of the church parade the Operation Christmas Child boxes up and place them on the chancel, where the pastor dedicates them to God and asks God's blessings to come to each child who will receive each box. Then we ship them to a central distribution center in North Carolina to be sent out around the world.

This past year, our congregation of 150 sent out 84 boxes, with 50 children participating in this project. Individual families or whole churches can participate in this project. Here's the address where you can write for more information about this project:

Samaritan's Purse
P.O. Box 3000
Boone, NC 28607
Phone: 828-262-1980; Fax 828-266-1053
E-mail: occinfo@samaritan.org
Website: www.samaritanspurse.org

✣ Activity 26: Needs and Wants Survey

*It is written: "Distribution was made as each had need" (Acts
4:35). By this we do not imply that there should be favoritism —
God forbid — but rather consideration for weaknesses. Whoever
needs less should thank God and not be distressed, but those who
need more should feel humble because of their weakness.*

— THE RULE OF ST. BENEDICT, chap. 34

How are parents to discern between needs and wants in the family? Every family must determine these boundaries for themselves.
Below you'll find a set of statements for family discussion on family needs and wants. If your children are early elementary age or
younger, you may want to hold these discussions between parents
or with close friends who are helping you to raise your children.

Needs and Wants Survey

Respond to each statement with one of the following evaluations:
strongly agree, agree, neutral, disagree, strongly disagree. Then
discuss your responses with one another.

1. We often discuss the difference between needs and wants.

2. Our family has all it needs.

3. Our family enjoys some luxuries (wants).

4. Our family knows the difference between needs and wants.

5. We have studied the Bible together concerning material possessions and wealth.

6. The Bible has truths and principles to teach us about needs and wants.

7. We are instructing our children about money: giving, saving, and spending.

8. We have a family budget for giving, saving, and spending.

9. Our family enjoys giving to others.

10. We have local charities and national or international missions which we support.

11. We have seen poverty face to face.

12. We know people who are poor.

13. We have taken regular steps toward simplifying our lifestyle.

14. We have read books on creative ways to live more simply.

15. We have served the needy in our community in some way.

16. Sometimes we feel the pinch of not having enough.

17. There is nothing virtuous about being poor.

18. There is nothing virtuous about being rich.

19. We have enough food, adequate shelter, clean drinking water, basic medical care.

20. True poverty is the poverty we discover in our spirits before God.

21. We are poor.

22. True wealth is found in Christ through worship, Scripture, and prayer, not in what we own.

23. We are wealthy.

24. We regularly spend quality time as a family doing simple things together.

25. We know in our home, "the grace of our Lord Jesus Christ, that though he was rich, yet for your sakes he became poor, so that you through his poverty might become rich." (2 Corinthians 8:9)

Especially in light of the information about world events we receive daily through instant global telecommunications, we owe it to our children and their children to take steps out of our well-padded, materialistic bubble and creatively serve a world in need. In our materialistic culture my wife and I have wrestled plenty over how to raise spiritually minded children, meeting their needs without indulging their material wants. Raising nonmaterialistic children who are grateful for God's gift of life is one of our greatest parenting challenges.

For Further Study

Foster, Richard. *Freedom of Simplicity.* San Francisco: Harper-SanFrancisco, 1989.

Longacre, Doris Janzen. *Living More with Less.* Scottdale, Pa.: Herald Press, 1980.

St. James, Elaine. *Simplify Your Life with Kids: 1001 Ways to Make Family Life Easier and More Fun.* Kansas City, Mo.: Andrews McMeel Publishing, 1997.

✠ Activity 27: Sponsor a Child

> Religion that God our Father accepts as pure and faultless
> is this: to look after orphans and widows in their distress.
>
> —James 1:27

Ever since Jesus rebuked his first disciples for hindering children from coming to him, the followers of Christ have offered creative compassion to children. Among the many aids to children begun by Christ's followers, you find orphanages, schools, hospitals, adoption agencies, books, literacy programs, and immunization clinics. Benedictine monasteries welcomed unwanted children and offered them food, shelter, education, and a caring community. As Benedict describes this ministry, *although human nature itself is inclined to be compassionate toward the elderly and the young, the authority of the rule should also provide for them* (RB, 37).

In the twentieth century, Christians again discovered a creative approach to helping "orphans in their distress": child sponsorships. "Sponsor a Child" programs match families in wealthy realms of the world with needy children in poor places.

Over the past two decades, our family has actively sponsored several children, either as a family or through our local congregation. The concept is simple: pledge a certain amount of financial and prayer support each month to a certain agency. The amount varies from agency to agency. See below for details. The agency sends you a sponsorship brochure, featuring a needy child somewhere in the world. You receive a photo of your sponsored child, a handwritten letter from your child and a translation of the letter, and a brief biography of your child. Throughout the year, letters and photos may be exchanged. Through your direct financial support, a needy child receives food, medical aid, educational support, and the wonderful assurance that someone in the world cares.

Sponsor-a-Child Agencies

Compassion International
Colorado Springs, CO 80997
Phone: 719-594-9900 or
800-336-7676;
E-mail: ciinfo@us.ci.org
Website: www.compassion.org

Founded in early 1950s; sponsors over 300,000 children in twenty-two countries; child sponsorship costs: $28/month.

World Vision
34834 Weyerhaeuser Way South
Federal Way, WA 98001
Phone: 888-511-6592
Website: www.worldvision.org

Founded in 1950 by Bob Pierce; sponsors over one million children worldwide; child sponsorship costs: $26/month.

✢ Activity 28: DEAR Time – Drop Everything And Read

Reading will always accompany the meals.
— THE RULE OF ST. BENEDICT, chap. 38

Benedict united mealtime with oral reading. To this day, you hear books being read aloud during meals at Benedictine monasteries. In the wisdom of Benedict, books are viewed as food for the soul and listening to good books being read a necessary part of a monk's daily diet.

You will find this same practice in many public schools today: time set aside daily for reading of books. Our children have grown up through public schools with DEAR time: Drop Everything And Read. Just this year, our local high school instituted a mandatory school-wide policy of twenty minutes a day for DEAR time. When I commended my friend Doug Dougherty, our school superintendent, for taking this step, he told me that studies have shown the most effective way to improve literacy is through regular time for reading. Good books are food for the mind and soul. Establish healthy reading habits early on, and they will feed the family through years and generations. If your family does not currently read aloud on at least a weekly basis, try the following activity as a new way to enjoy family time together.

When your children have outgrown naps, develop the household habit of a quiet reading time.

✤ Collect suggestions from each family member of book titles to be read aloud at DEAR time.

✤ Commit yourselves to a set amount of time each week, on a set night of the week for DEAR time. For example, "Our family promises to read aloud every Thursday evening for thirty minutes, just before bedtime."

✤ Begin your DEAR time with a fun book that catches everyone's attention: go to your local library with your book list from the family meeting and ask the librarian to offer you suggestions for a good read aloud book for your family, given the ages of your children. There are many books available that offer helpful book lists for parents seeking books to read aloud to their children.

✤ Choose someone in the family who likes to read aloud. Share reading duties with various members of the family. Benedict encouraged the choice of a reader who had the *ability to benefit their hearers.*

✤ Do not allow children to walk around, talk, play, or otherwise disrupt the reader. This is "Drop Everything And Read" time. Benedict warned: *Let there be complete silence. No whispering, no speaking — only the reader's voice should be heard there* (RB, 38).

✤ If you've never had a read aloud time in your home before, begin with a short time, five to ten minutes, and read a picture book or a short chapter of a chapter book, depending on the age of your children.

✤ Better to finish the DEAR time with your children wanting more than to bore them to distraction. We try to read daily to our teenage sons for thirty minutes, just before bedtime.

✤ Over the years, broaden your children's reading diet. William Kilpatrick, in his *Books That Build Character*, offers an excellent book list with brief descriptions of books in the following categories: Picture Books; Fables and Fairy Tales; Myths, Legends, and Folktales; Sacred Texts; Books for Holidays and Holy Days; Historical Fiction; Contemporary Fiction; Fantasy and Science Fiction; and Biography. Keep expanding your children's vocabulary, imagination, and horizons through time together in good books.

✤ Read aloud regularly from the Bible, God's Word and our soul's finest feast!

✠ Activity 29: Birds and Bees – Talking with Your Child about Sex

Each man has his own gift from God; one has this gift, another has that.   — 1 Corinthians 7:7

Children need to learn three basic lessons about sex. Sex is sacred. Sex is risky. Sex is good. In the spirit of Benedict, these lessons are learned in the midst of daily life as we face ordinary events. When the time comes in parenting to sit down together and have a face-to-face "sex talk" with our children, what do we say? How do we teach our children about sex? Most parents struggle with sex education in the home, unsure if we're doing it right, if our children are learning what they need to know about this mysterious aspect of life. What are we supposed to tell our children about sex?

We can tell our children that sex is sacred. Sex is God's idea. Sex is holy, not dirty. Sex is good, not bad. Sex is a gift from God, not merely a basic bodily instinct. Because sex is sacred, we enjoy sex within the sacred relationship of the covenant of marriage. God designed sex for marriage. Three times in Scripture we hear this truth about sexual union. "For this reason a man will leave his father and mother and be united to his wife, and they will become one flesh" (see Genesis 2:24; Matthew 19:5; Ephesians 5:31). Jesus and Paul reaffirm the teaching of Genesis concerning sacred sex. Jesus adds the warning, "They are no longer two, but one. Therefore what God has joined together, let man not separate" (Matthew 19:6). I pronounce this solemn warning at every wedding I perform. The act of sexual intercourse is a holy mystery created by God to join two people, a husband and a wife, together into one new creation.

Only within the covenant of marriage, one man with one woman, can a couple know the fullness of God's blessing in sexual union. Any sexual intercourse outside of this covenant is outside of God's blessing. Premarital sex, extramarital sex, and abusive sex: these are common in our world today. They are not God's design for sex union.

All sex is risky. Those who engage in sex outside God's design greatly increase their risks. The risk list is long: sexually transmitted diseases, HIV/AIDS, unwanted pregnancy, abortion, infertility, divorce, family break-ups, infidelity, broken trust, sexual abuse, rape, incest, addiction to pornography, prostitution, and the list goes on. These are the themes we read about in our newspapers, watch nightly on our televisions, and pay to see in our local movie houses. Sex is big business. Sex sells. The world of advertising exploits sex to sell products. People exploit sex for personal short-term pleasure, power, and profit. Any way about it, sex is risky. How do we teach our children about sex in such a world?

Vows. We give our children the gift of vows. When I meet with couples who are about to be married I help them write their vows and teach couples how to live within vows. Benedict offered Western civilization a great gift when he called monks to take a lifelong vow of stability. *The one to be received, however, must first promise his stability, fidelity to the monastic lifestyle, and obedience before all* (RB, 58). Marriage is such a vow, a vow of stability, and a commitment between a man and a woman to be faithful to one another for life. The Bible clearly declares that sexual intercourse is for people who are living under the vow of stability, the covenant of marriage.

Our culture tells us that sex is for consenting adults. As long as both partners agree, it says, sex is a basic right and an animal need for human adults. Get it where you can find it. Get it as often as you can. There are no boundaries or rules or vows necessary except mutual consent. No marriage covenant is needed. Just find another consenting adult. Gender is not the issue. Satisfy your desires. Fulfill your passions. Get sex. This is what our sexual culture seems to offer our children. How do we educate our kids about sex in such a culture? Here are some practical ideas for sex education in the family cloister.

Twelve Ideas for Talking with Your Children about Sex

1. Take your children to marriage ceremonies and talk together about marriage vows. Tell your children about marriage, about living under vows, and about God's gift of the covenant marriage.

2. Read and study the first two chapters of Genesis together as a family every year. With preschool and early elementary age children, get a children's Bible with pictures for this time together.

3. Pray with your children for God's blessing: for growth in physical development, emotional maturity, and spiritual wisdom in God's Word. As a model for growth, refer to Luke 2:52: "And Jesus grew in wisdom and stature, and in favor with God and men." Ask God to help your children grow in wisdom, in stature, and in favor with God and others.

4. Teach your children correct names for male-female body parts, and use these names when talking about personal hygiene.

5. Help children to appreciate God's handiwork, seeing all of creation, including our bodies, as God's creativity and blessing.

6. Discover "teachable moments" in which to talk with your children about sex and help your children discover more of God's beautiful design for sexuality. An example: I listen to National Public Radio news in the car in the afternoon. Often, my teenage sons are with me after I pick them up from sports practice. As reports come on the radio that concern sexual issues or stories related to sexuality, I take time to discuss these issues with my boys, ask for their views, and share my convictions on the subject.

7. Study nature together: seeds, eggs, cells, fertilization, reproduction, birth, male and female differences in creation. Through ordinary conversation about such elements in nature, talk with your children about these elements in boys and girls, in dads and moms.

8. Study picture books together about bodies, physical development, how we are made.

9. Offer simple, straightforward, age-appropriate answers to your children's questions about bodies, about sex, about where babies come from, about birth. Get involved in your children's education at school when they are going over reproduction and sexuality. Review the materials handed out to use them to instruct your children about their own development.

10. Teach your children your morals and biblical values about sex. In 2000, the *New York Times* published results of a teen survey about sex education. When asked, "What was the most helpful kind of sex education your parents provided in the home?" a majority of teens responded, "They shared their own convictions, morals, and values concerning sex."

This is especially important as profane examples show up on television, in movies, on billboards, in school conversations, or from other influences. We can't shield our children from all misinformation and corrosive influences with regard to sexuality. But a parent can develop a child's moral character and spiritual maturity to face sexual temptations with integrity and to discover God's way of sexual purity. As Paul writes, "Do not conform any longer to the pattern of this world, but be transformed by the renewing of your mind. Then you will be able to test and approve what God's will is — his good, pleasing, and perfect will" (Romans 12:2).

11. Provide your children with mature role models. Ask couples or individuals who are older and wiser than you are to spend time with your children, to get to know them and invest their lives and faith in your family life. Paul describes his relationship with Timothy as "my true son in the faith" (1 Timothy 1:2). Paul mentored Timothy as a spiritual father mentors a son in the faith. As parents, we are wise to help our children find spiritual fathers and mothers in the faith.

12. Be merciful with your children when they disappoint you and make mistakes. Forgive them and discipline them with compassion, mindful of your own failures and troubles, remembering God's unfailing love. As James declares, "Mercy triumphs over judgment!" (James 2:13)

✠ Activity 30: World Hunger Project

Is not this the kind of fasting I have chosen: to loose the chains of injustice and untie the cords of the yoke, to set the oppressed free and break every yoke? Is it not to share your food with the hungry and to provide the poor wanderer with shelter?   —Isaiah 58:6–7

With television and the Internet, hungry people in our world come right into our homes and ask for our help. This is both a blessing and a curse. Blessings flow into our lives whenever our hearts are moved by what moves God's heart. The heart of God moves with compassion toward those who suffer. When we allow our hearts and actions to be moved with compassion for those who suffer, we will live rich and blessed lives. The curse comes from feeling inadequate, guilty, overwhelmed, or perhaps just numb or apathetic as a result of seeing too much suffering and doing too little about it.

World hunger devours families and children in every corner of the world. The statistics are staggering. The World Health Organization estimates that one-third of the world is well fed, one-third is underfed, and one-third is starving. Children suffer most. Over one-half of childhood deaths around the world are hunger-related. World hunger relief agencies estimate that 12–15 million children die every year of hunger-related causes. That translates to over 32,000 children dying every day worldwide because they don't have enough to eat.

What can a family do to help when the problem is so overwhelming and often times so far away? Benedict would encourage us to build a bridge into needy people's lives through the spiritual discipline of fasting. He calls all monks in the monastic family to practice fasting on a regular basis. Lent is the six-week season of penance and fasting leading up to Easter. Besides during Lent, monks fast throughout the year as an expression of their desire for God.

> *The life of a monastic ought to be a continuous Lent.... In other*
> *words, let each one deny themselves some food, drink, sleep, need-*
> *less talking, and idle jesting, and look forward to holy Easter with*
> *joy and spiritual longing.* (RB, 49)

The spiritual discipline of fasting not only purifies our lives and unites us closer to God. Fasting unites our lives with hungry people in the world and brings blessings back upon our heads. As the prophet Isaiah boldly declares, "If you spend yourselves in behalf of the hungry and satisfy the needs of the oppressed, then your light will rise in the darkness, and your night will become like the noonday. The LORD will guide you always; he will satisfy your needs . . . and will strengthen your frame" (Isaiah 58:6–7, 10–11).

World Hunger Project

At least once a year invite your family to participate in a World Hunger Project. Here's how it works.

✣ Set time aside for your World Hunger Project. Plan for a week-long celebration. Though we haven't done this in our family, I've planned such a project for college students when I served as a campus pastor. The World Hunger Project lasted a whole week, during which we provided ways to interact with our hungry world.

✣ Invite the family to fast. Instead of abstinence from food, offer the family a different kind of fast: abstinence from luxury activities or foods for a week. Here are a few possibilities: fast from watching television; stop playing electronic games; give up time on the computer and the Internet; write letters instead of calling people by phone; go without fast food or candy. Televisions, video games, computers, phones, and fast food are luxuries in most parts of the world.

✟ During your World Hunger Project, focus your family instead upon alternative activities:

> Enjoy family devotions.
>
> Read Bible passages on God's provision and care for the needy.
>
> Watch a video available through a world hunger relief agency.
>
> Study world hunger.
>
> Read stories of needy people in our world.
>
> Get out a globe or world map and learn about the geography of hunger.
>
> Write letters to elected officials expressing your concern about world hunger.
>
> Pray for God's blessing to come to those who suffer from hunger and malnutrition.

✟ Catholic Relief Services offers a world hunger project called Operation Rice Bowl. "For 25 years, Operation Rice Bowl has been bringing families, parishes, schools and other faith communities together during the Lenten Season to pray, fast, learn, and give. . . . Through daily reflection, prayer, and action, Operation Rice Bowl helps you connect with your global community." For more information contact: Catholic Relief Services, 209 West Fayette Street, Baltimore, MD 21201; tel.: 410-625-2220 or 800-235-2772; website: www.catholicrelief.org.

✚ Ask every family member to contribute toward your "World Hunger Fund." Send off a check to a hunger relief agency for world hunger relief.

✚ At the end of the week, celebrate a "Third-World" meal: eat a dinner of beans and rice.

As families share in the adventure of fasting, God will share with you the joy of the Holy Spirit, the love of Christ for all who suffer, and the hope of the holy feast to come.

Chapter Five

ACTIVITIES FOR FAMILY LIFE TOGETHER

By this all men will know that you are my disciples, if you love one another.   —John 13:35

Family community does not come naturally or easily. The family cloister must work together over years to unwrap this God-given gift.   —*The Family Cloister,* 118

When I enrolled in college, there were always more courses I wanted to take than I was able to fit into my schedule. At the University of Washington, I pored over the course list (a book that looked like a small town phone directory) and wrote down every course I wanted to take. Then I would start paring away, selecting five or six classes out of the thirty or forty classes on my list. I never did take Sanskrit, the History of the Celtic Peoples, Thermodynamics, Fencing, Screenplay Writing, or Poetry of Medieval Saints. I did get around to taking Circus Skills Workshop, Jazz Composition, Children's Theater, and Newspaper Feature Writing. I could have been a professional student for decades.

Since leaving graduate school, I've enrolled in the college of parenting. Over the past two decades, we've taken dozens of "courses" together as a family. Some of these must be taken by correspondence now that our firstborn is in college. Some we've never completed. Some are ongoing, lifelong extension classes.

Families are little schools in which we learn God's holy lessons of love: Family Scheduling, Confession and Accountability, Work Habits and Study Skills, Family Creativity, Playing and Praying Together. These are just some of the courses offered in what Benedict calls *a school for God's service* (RB, Prologue). The classes below are a sampling of ways to build fun and growth into your daily life together as a family.

✛ *Activity 31: The Family Schedule*

It is the responsibility of the abbot and prioress to announce, day and night, the hour for the Opus Dei. They may do so personally or delegate the responsibility to a conscientious member, so that everything may be done at the proper time.

— THE RULE OF ST. BENEDICT, chap. 47

Every monastery I've visited posts its monastic schedule for all guests to read. We also post our family schedules on a bulletin board on the wall in our dining room, next to the family phone, where everyone has easy access to the information. My wife and I both work. Our teenage sons are involved with school, sports, and various other extracurricular activities. We rely upon our family schedule to order our week.

About once a year, we gather together all the various schedules for our family: school schedules, sporting practices and game

schedules, church activities, work schedules, dentist, orthodon-
tist, and doctor schedules, chore charts, club meeting times,
service groups, and any other schedules we have. A few years
ago, all three of our children were playing soccer on different
teams. Almost every day of the week for fifteen weeks required
some kind of soccer activity, a practice or a game. Often games
and practices would overlap. I put these schedules on the computer and went day by day, planning who had to be where
and when.

My wife and I sit together once a month for schedule planning.
We fill in dates, times, and events on a master calendar and discuss
together family priorities for the upcoming few weeks. We try to
set aside certain evenings or days for regular family time together.

At a family meeting, we present the Family Schedule, asking
for input from our kids. Depending on the ages of your children,
alter your family schedule according to the ideas shared at the
family meeting.

Then we post the Family Schedule and regularly refer to this
master calendar. For example, in the morning, we go over major
events, pick-up times, sports practices, and anything out of the
ordinary. We also try to announce family times: "Tonight, we'll
all have dinner at 6 P.M. and we have a special family surprise
planned after dinner."

As new events come up, we consult the Family Schedule. One
of our biggest challenges we've faced as parents has been keeping
the balance between family time together and family time apart,
between time at home and time away. Whenever we begin to get
a handle on this delicate balance, changes happen in our growing
family that make us laugh and scratch our heads as we head back
one more time to the Family Schedule drawing board.

✤ Activity 32: Family Portraits

At a family fun night, try drawing family portraits. Children often express their inner lives through art more clearly than with words. Though this activity is designed as a creative, fun-filled activity, we are wise to listen to what our children are telling us about their lives through the various means available.

✤ Give every member of the family a piece of drawing paper and have on hand markers, crayons, and colored pencils.

✤ Ask everyone to draw a picture of the family with every member in the family doing something.

✤ "Show and Tell" once everyone is finished. Let each family member talk about his or her family portrait. No negative critiques of anyone's portrait are allowed. This family activity is intended to give insight into how members of the family see the family at this moment in time.

✤ After all the family portraits have been drawn and shared, display them in the "Family Art Gallery," on a wall in your home where other family artwork is displayed.[11]

✤ Activity 33: Laundry Day

Doing laundry in a family household is like dealing with mistakes in a family. How foolish it would be to expect clothes never to get soiled. We make mistakes and end up in the mud.... There is a quiet joy and contentment in accepting the lifelong daily task of doing laundry. In the same manner we attend to mistakes within the family cloister.

— *The Family Cloister,* 126

Every Saturday is laundry day in our house. Okay, that's not quite true. The washer and dryer run almost every day of the week. But on Saturday, all laundry reports to the laundry room. We've been working for years with our children on how to care for their clothes. They are now all teenagers and fully capable of doing their own laundry. Or at least, that's the hope. The real story is our children still expect mom to do all their laundry. Children learn much better when a chore is treated like a game. When we treat laundry like another boring task week after week, the task will fall to adults 95 percent of the time. Here's an alternative.

How to Play the Laundry Game

✤ After Saturday morning breakfast, put march music on the stereo or CD player. I grew up with the marches of John Philip Sousa playing on Saturday mornings. I also marched as drum major of my high school marching band. March music still motivates me, helping me tackle unpleasant tasks like Saturday chores. Select music for your household that will get the family in the groove for cleaning up.

✤ With the music playing, march over to a child. Arm in arm with your child, march to their bedroom, collect all their dirty clothes, and march together into the laundry room.

✤ Deposit the dirty clothes into heaps (or laundry hampers, depending on your style). Go through the steps and instructions for separating clothes with each child.

✤ While one child is separating out colors and whites, march off to collect the next child and his or her laundry.

✤ When all the laundry is collected and separated, begin to run loads.

✤ As each load finishes, offer your child a small incentive to transfer the load from washer to dryer, or to remove the load from dryer. Allow a trip to the cookie jar, the fruit snack bowl, or the hard-candy container.

✤ Once clothes are dry and lying in a pile, put on another piece of music, place the warm pile of clean clothes on the living room couch, and fold clothes together with that child.

✤ See that the children carry their load of folded clothes back to their rooms and get help putting their folded clothes away properly.

✤ After the children are finished with their Laundry Game, reward them with a spin of the Laundry Spinner or a roll of the Laundry Dice. Allow your laundry helpers to pick something out of the Laundry Treasure Chest depending on their spin or roll. Of course, this means having a variety of small inexpensive toys, school supplies (colored pencils, erasers, markers), or nonperishable treats on hand, number coded one through six, and placed in a decorated box or small chest.

✤ After a few years of playing the Laundry Game with your family, you will have trained your children not only how to wash their own clothes, but how to "whistle while you work" and enjoy the game of cleaning up after themselves.

✤ Activity 34: The Fix-It Shop

> *If monastics commit a fault while at any work — while working in the kitchen, in the storeroom, in serving, in the bakery, in the garden, in any craft, or anywhere else — either by breaking or losing something or failing in any other way in any other place, they must at once come before the prioress or abbot and community and of their own accord admit their fault and make satisfaction.*   — THE RULE OF ST. BENEDICT, chap. 46

While building a horse corral, my dad sent me off to his tool shop to fetch the "board-stretcher." I was seven years old and thrilled to be Dad's helper. I looked and looked. Dad had described the tool to me. When I returned empty-handed, I found my dad smiling. "Just couldn't find that board-stretcher?" I've been hunting for the right tool ever since. Though a retired engineer, Dad has always kept current his "jerry-built" license (the official permission to build or fix things incorrectly without the right tool or materials). His disordered workbench was well stocked with tools and only he could find the right one.

Benedict knew that wherever there was work to be done there would be things that needed to be fixed. People break things. Things wear out. Families are little science laboratories, proving over and over the law of entropy: things fall apart, break down, erode, corrode, wind down, rot, decompose, rust, and generally make life difficult.

For Benedict, the broken place is also the grace place. Within the broken family, grace is revealed in the act of confession, by admitting our faults to one another. Put another way, spiritual families live honestly with one another, bringing into the open offences or wrongdoings. When we break something we fess up.

Try another role-play discussion to engage the family in facing family situations where something breaks or gets lost.

The Family Fix-It Shop: A Family Role-Play and Discussion

Call the family together for a family discussion on "Breaking and Fixing." Act out one of the role-play stories below. The cast of characters includes Dad, Mom, Sister, and Brother. Alter the cast and the story to better fit your situation.

1. **The Broken Cup:** Dad accidentally knocks a cup off the counter, breaking it. Daughter sees him do it. Dad tells Daughter, "Don't tell anyone. Mom will be upset." The cup was Mom's favorite, made by one of her children in a pottery class. Mom comes in to get a cup of tea and asks if anyone knows where her favorite cup is.

2. **The Peace Rose:** Brother and Sister are playing soccer in the backyard. The soccer ball hits a rose bush and breaks off some branches with rose buds. Brother and Sister know they will get in trouble if they admit to kicking the soccer ball into the rose bush. They discuss their options: (1) hide the broken off branches and hope Mom won't notice; (2) admit they did it and buy a new rose plant as a "peace offering."

3. **Faded Blue Jeans:** Mom spills bleach on Son's favorite blue jeans, ruining them. She considers trying to bleach them completely, throwing them away, blaming it on Son, or confessing what she did and offering to get him a new pair of pants of his choice. Son finds out from Daughter. He is very angry; he wanted to wear those pants to a friend's house tonight. Mom becomes defensive, saying Son can just learn

to do his own laundry if he's going to be so mean. Daughter plays peace-maker.

4. **Computer Problems:** Sister has accidentally erased Brother's five-page project on the computer. She was in a hurry to shut down the computer, after spending too much time instant-messaging with her friends. Mom had gotten upset and was coming up to turn off the computer herself if Daughter didn't get off immediately. The computer is now off. It suddenly dawns on Sister that she failed to save someone's document in the process of shutting down the computer. Later that evening, Brother asks if anyone knows what happened to his term paper on the computer. He can't find it anywhere. Sister remains silent until confronted. She blames Mom. Brother blames Sister. They get into a fight. Mom shouts, telling Son and Daughter to stop yelling at each other.

5. **Broken Binoculars:** Brother and Sister take Dad's binoculars without permission. They go outside, climb a tree, and pass the binoculars back and forth to get a good look around the neighborhood. The binoculars accidentally drop and the lenses break. Brother and Sister discuss what to do now. Brother is in favor of burying the binoculars in the yard and telling no one. Sister wants to put them back and hope no one will notice they are broken or not accuse them if they do notice. Mom calls out from the house asking if everything is all right.

✣ Discuss what happened and how to "fix it."

✣ Ask for family ideas and input on basic rules for the family when things get broken or lost.

✣ Write out these basic "rules of the house" in a family journal.

✤ Refer to these "fix-it" rules as issues come up and the family needs ways to creatively and positively fix broken relationships, deal with lost or broken material possessions, and handle other family difficulties.

✤ Activity 35: Study Time

With his commitment to study, Benedict quietly revolutionized Western society. Every monk was required to learn to read and write. Manuscripts were copied and recopied, making available enough books for daily reading within the cloister. From these seedlings of study grew some of the great trees of Western civilization: libraries, schools, universities, and increased literacy among the common population. Study stretches the mind, soul, and spirit, to better understand God, people, and creation. — *The Family Cloister, 129–30*

There are a variety of ways to study in the family. We believe every day is a study day, every day is a day for learning, reading, growing in body, mind, and spirit. We also believe that education starts in the home. We do not send our children off to public schools because we expect the school to teach our children everything they need to know. We believe that formal education serves to complement daily home education through the daily discipline of study, including meditation, reading, Bible study, journaling, and nature study.

Meditation

✤ Sit alone, removed from distractions.

✤ Open the Bible and read a passage of Scripture.

✣ Listen to the Word of God, personally speaking to you.

✣ Memorize a phrase or sentence from the Bible.

✣ Give your full attention to God, breathing in God's goodness.

✣ Teach your children to listen to God through meditation.

Reading

✣ Take regular trips with children to the local library, encouraging them to pick out good books to read.

✣ Provide time each day for reading: reading alone and reading aloud.

✣ Read age-appropriate stories to your children.

✣ Give them books for their birthdays.

✣ Reward them when they finish reading another book.

Sacred Reading

✣ Learn to practice *Lectio Divina,* or "Sacred Reading."

✣ Climb up the four rungs of the ladder of "Sacred Reading": Read, Pray, Meditate, and Contemplate.

✣ As you read the Bible or a spiritual classic, allow the truths and divine insights to shine light into your soul, to wash over your spirit.

✣ Pause when a particular phrase stands out to you. Mull that phrase over. Offer this truth up to God in gratitude.

✣ Proceed slowly, going deeper into your life with God through "Sacred Reading."

Bible Reading and Bible Study

✤ Read the Bible daily, in the morning and at night.

✤ Use a daily Bible reading guide, and stay with a Bible reading plan for a year.

✤ Study the Bible using the REAP Method:

   R *Read:* read a passage of God's Word.

   E *Examine:* ask what the author is saying, what are the themes, events, principles.

   A *Apply:* ask what God is saying to you through this passage.

   P *Pray and Practice:* ask God to transform your life as you live in obedience to God's Word.

Journaling

✤ Buy a journal for each child and for parents: inexpensive spiral notebooks work very well.

✤ Keep a record of poems, ideas, prayers, dreams, Bible passages, new insights, hopes, troubles, new commitments or resolutions, and God's answers to your prayers.

✤ Encourage children to draw pictures of God and of Bible stories.

✤ Encourage children to write out Scripture passages and prayers in their journals.

Nature Study

✤ Go on nature walks in every season.

✤ Collect little creatures in a bug box, terrarium, or aquarium.

✤ Grow a garden together.

✤ Try simple science experiments together.

✤ Invest in nature study tools: binoculars, rubber boots, a flower press, and books on spiders, camping gear, and the like.

✤ Encourage your children to "specialize" in a certain area of nature study for a whole year. Take a year with your six-year-old to help her learn all she can about butterflies. Take a whole year with your thirteen-year-old to learn all you can together about reproduction.

✤ Memorize your favorite poems, quotations, and Scripture passages about God's creation. One of our favorite quotations comes from the poem "God's Grandeur" by the English Jesuit priest Gerard Manley Hopkins:

> The world is charged with the grandeur of God.
> It will flame out, like shining from shook foil;
> It gathers to a greatness, like the ooze of oil
> Crushed. Why do men then now not reck his rod?[12]

✤ Activity 36: The Family Art Studio

If there are artisans in the monastery, they are to practice their craft with all humility.   — THE RULE OF ST. BENEDICT, chap. 57

Almost every room of our house is decorated with original artwork from friends and family. Included in this collection you'll discover weavings, quilts, watercolors, pen and ink sketches, pottery, blown glass, needlepoint, calligraphy, and children's drawings. When our children bring us their works of art, we try to spend time enjoying their creativity and then we place them in our "Family

Art Gallery," a dedicated wall in our home for our children's art. Two of my favorite pieces hang up above my pottery wheel, large primary color tempura self-portraits of our two younger sons.

Benedict encouraged the arts in the cloister. Through this little nudge by a spiritual leader in the early sixth century, art flourished through the Middle Ages. Included in monastic art you'll discover marvelous illuminations of Scripture manuscripts, sacred icons of biblical scenes, handcrafts such as pottery and fabric arts, cottage industries such as beekeeping and breadmaking, and the development of artisan guilds that practiced their creativity for the benefit of the whole community.

Try setting aside places in your home dedicated to creativity. Depending on the size of your home, several of these areas are better than just one. Place in these areas the tools and supplies for creative expression. I recently moved an empty chest of drawers into the "Mud Room" right next to my pottery wheel and dumped all my pottery tools and supplies into the drawers. We also have a drawer in our kitchen dedicated to baking arts with rolling pins, measuring cups, and other implements for creating artistic treats such as pies and loaves of bread.

In *The Family Cloister* I mention thirty-two types of creative expression in eight categories:

✣ writing, speaking, story-telling, dramatizing

✣ cooking, home-making, gardening, designing

✣ making melody, harmony, rhythm, and composing

✣ weaving, knitting, embroidering, sewing

✣ healing, mending, repairing, restoring

✣ acting, directing, dancing, choreography

✤ inventing, programming, translating, structuring

✤ role-playing, game-playing, laughter-making, delight-taking

Through such activities, the family cloister grows in God's grace. Over the years, you will add to your Family Art Gallery a beautiful collection of memories, creativity, and artistry.

✤ Activity 37: Hug o' War

> I will not play at tug o' war
> I'd rather play at hug o' war
> — SHEL SILVERSTEIN[13]

Many of the following ideas are drawn from *The Family Cloister,* from the chapter on "Play and Laughter" (136–37). Play and laughter are two qualities of life we value highly in our home.

Thirteen Ideas for Family Play and Laughter

1. Set aside daily time in the home for play. Children need lots of time for play: playing together with other children, playing alone, and playing with parents.

2. Make room in your home for play. Our kids have spent thousands of hours in Legotown, a bunk bed play area in our youngest son's bedroom.

3. Organize your children's play area with them, allowing their input for where things go and how they should be organized to enhance play.

4. Get on the same level as your children to play with them, a few minutes every day.

5. Commit several evenings each month for "Family Game Night." After a recent Friday evening family meeting, we all broke out into a housewide game of Hide and Go Seek, topped off with family sweet treat time.

6. Read funny stories aloud together.

7. Watch the classic comedians, like the Three Stooges or Charlie Chaplin, on TV and video.

8. Listen to comedy cassette tapes on longer drives as a family.

9. Develop inside family jokes that build family members up and draw upon family memories. One silly tradition we've added in just the last year is "The Dumb Joke of the Day." At dinner we recite dumb jokes we've heard during the day and choose together which is the dumbest. A recent example: Two parrots were sitting on a perch. One said to the other, "Do you smell fish?"

10. Find playful ways to communicate serious lessons and warnings. The medicine of discipline goes down much easier with "just a spoonful of sugar."

11. Develop creative ways to celebrate special days, such as birthdays and holidays. We love our birthday treasure hunts. At every birthday, the birthday boy is given his first clue. He must follow the clues around the house (or as they've gotten older, around the neighborhood or town), solving the riddles to get to his treasure, his presents. I make as many clues as they celebrate in years.

12. Play the "Hah! Hah! Hah!" Game. Here's how: (1) One family member, we'll call him or her "Funny Bones," lies down. (2) The next lies down with his or her head on the

first person's tummy. (3) The next person lies down with his head on the second person's tummy, until every family member is lying down, connected head to tummy. (4) "Funny Bones" says "Hah!" (5) The next person says "Hah! Hah!" (6) The next person says "Hah! Hah! Hah!," all the way down the line or around the circle until the whole family is giggling and laughing.

13. Touch! We tickle, play "gotch'ya last," wrestle on the carpet, hug each other when we come home, kiss one another good-night. Our bodies are designed by God to offer us pleasure and delight.

✛ Activity 38: Writing a Family Prayer

Those who have been sent on a journey are not to omit the prescribed hours [of prayer] but to observe them as best they can, not neglecting their measure of service.

— THE RULE OF ST. BENEDICT, chap. 50

Early in our marriage, we wrote words for a travel prayer and have sung this prayer every time we head out on a long trip. Every member of the family knows this prayer by heart. Try writing a Family Prayer to use at meal times, at bedtimes, at times when a member of the family is going away on a trip. Many anthologies of childhood prayers are available. Check out one of these collections from your area library and use it as a reference for writing your own Family Prayer. After you write your Family Prayer get everyone in the family to memorize the prayer. Pray this prayer at mealtime, at bedtime, and as family members go away on trips.

Writing a Family Prayer

✤ Call the family together and provide pencils and paper for everyone.

✤ Describe the activity and its purpose: to write a prayer the entire family can offer to God at a meal, at bedtime, at the coming and going of family members, in times of crisis.

✤ Pass around ideas of prayers from the Bible and from other written prayers. Here are a few of our favorites:

Psalm 75:1
We give thanks to Thee, O God, we give thanks,
we give thanks to Thee, O God, we give thanks,
for Thy Name is near,
Thy wondrous works men declare,
We give thanks to Thee, O God, we give thanks. (NASB)

Table Blessing
For health and strength and daily food,
We praise Thy name, O Lord.

Johnny Appleseed Prayer
O the Lord is good to me, and so I thank the Lord,
For giving me the things I need,
The sun and the rain and the appleseed,
The Lord is good to me.

St. Patrick's Prayer
Christ beside me, Christ before me, Christ behind me,
Christ within me, Christ beneath me, Christ above me.
Christ on my right hand, Christ on my left,
Christ where I lie, Christ where I sit, Christ where I rise.
Christ in the hearts of all who think of me,

Christ in the mouths of all who speak to me,
Christ in every eye that sees me,
Christ in every ear that hears me.

House Blessing Prayer
Be present at our table Lord,
Be here and everywhere adored,
These mercies bless and grant that we,
May strengthened for Thy service be.

St. Richard of Chichester
Day by day, dear Lord,
Of Thee, three things I pray:
To see Thee more clearly,
To love Thee more dearly,
To follow Thee more nearly,
Day by day.[14]

✢ Allow time for writing prayers. Encourage every family member to write at least a sentence prayer.

✢ Have each family member read his or her written prayers.

✢ Collect the family prayers together into a single prayer. Choose one family member to act as the "Scribe," the person in charge of writing down family ideas for the Family Prayer.

✢ After the Scribe writes down a prayer idea from every family member, get ideas from the family about rewording, editing, or reorganizing the prayer.

✢ Read aloud the Family Prayer. Though the length doesn't matter, try to keep it under fifty words.

✤ Give family members an opportunity to offer any last changes or suggestions. When all agree upon the Family Prayer, have the Scribe write it out.

✤ Gather together and pray the Family Prayer together, dedicating the Family Prayer and your family life together to God.

Chapter Six

ACTIVITIES FOR FAMILY HOSPITALITY

Offer hospitality to one another without grumbling.

— 1 Peter 4:9

Recently I stayed late at the church building to be hospitable toward a few community musicians who rehearse weekly in the church fellowship hall. I offered them a place to store their two tympani in one of the church storerooms. In return, the community symphony director and two other musicians offered to perform on violin, viola, and tympani at as many worship services as I would like. It is true what Hugh Feiss, O.S.B., writes in *Essential Monastic Wisdom:* "Hospitable people have more fun. They meet Christ in the strangest guises."[15]

Hospitality in the family cloister requires a choice: to keep the front door locked or to reach out beyond the members of the immediate family to welcome others as Christ. Benedict unveiled a remarkable faith understanding of hospitality when he wrote, *All guests who present themselves are to be welcomed as Christ, who said: "I was a stranger and you welcomed me"* (RB, 53).

The daily work of hospitality presents a family with what I believe to be one of the most delightful and challenging adventures a family can imagine. When we shut our doors to this adventure we shut the door of our family to God's mercy. Offer hospitality in Jesus' name in your family and discover together the wonders of God's promise, that "God will meet all your needs according to his glorious riches in Christ Jesus" (Philippians 4:19).

✦ Activity 39: Team Hospitality

Our sons have all played team sports since they were just barely able to kick a ball. I love team sports! What great lessons we've learned together through the seasons of soccer, basketball, swimming, and track. What wonderful lessons we can teach our children as we coach them in the "sport of hospitality."

Our little beach village plays team hospitality quite well. Anyone who visits our coastal resort will inevitably come in contact with at least a dozen people who focus their professional lives on hospitality: hotel desk clerks, maids, hostesses, waitresses, shop owners, gardeners, park rangers, and even the local pastor. We all work together to provide support to anyone who comes to the coast for refreshment. Of course, the main work belongs to God, who alone can renew our body, mind, and spirit.

The family is also such a little village, where others come for refreshment in body, mind, and spirit. Here are a few ideas for training the Hospitality Team for this vital calling.

✦ Divide up the hospitality tasks among each family member. It is important that every family member is given a place on the Hospitality Team. Here are some possible positions on the Hospitality Team:

The Greeter: welcomes people at the door, asks to take coat and hat.

Host/Hostess: offers guests something to drink or eat depending on the occasion.

Table Setter: helps set the table for a meal, lights candles.

Music and Fun: selects music for arrival and for meals; prepares fun activities for family.

Childcare Provider: takes care of little ones, providing age appropriate activities.

Linens and Towels: puts out sets of clean towels and puts clean linens on beds.

Kitchen Patrol: helps clear away dishes and cleans up kitchen after meal.

Prayer and Devotionals: offers to pray at meal times and leads morning devotions.

✤ Train each person in their tasks, with set times for practicing the skills of hospitality.

✤ Invite good friends over for a practice night, where everyone can try out their skills as members of the Hospitality Team.

✤ After the evening is over, offer praise and encouragement to the children for their part in offering hospitality.

✤ Keep stretching the family with different hospitality challenges: a weekend guest, a neighborhood party, a summer with an exchange student, an elderly member of the family for a season. Each of these decisions can be made together as a team, with parents acting as player-coach, providing guidance in the process.

✤ Before each experience of hospitality, share a brief prayer together, asking God's blessings to be with each person who comes into your home. Offer a simple prayer, "Lord, let us meet you in the face of these guests who come to our home. Bless us all with your great compassion, in Christ's name, Amen."

✤ Activity 40: The Gratitude Jar

Greed demands more and more, never satisfied with what is given.
Gratitude takes quiet delight in God's good gifts.
Greed shouts;
Gratitude listens.
Greed forces its way;
Gratitude willingly walks with another along their way.
Greed cripples and imprisons;
Gratitude heals and frees.

— *The Family Cloister,* 146

Find a large jar with a lid. Cut a slit in the lid. Place a hand-colored sign on the jar that reads, "The Gratitude Jar." For one whole year, beginning in January, try the gratitude experiment. Invite family members to think of one thing every day for which they are grateful. At dinner, enjoy a round of gratitude, going around the table, saying, "Today I'm grateful for...." Place a quarter in the jar for each statement of gratitude. Have on hand a supply of quarters for younger children who don't yet handle money. For older chil-

dren with an allowance or income from odd jobs, expect them
to place their own money into the Gratitude Jar. At Christmas
time, open the Gratitude Jar as a family, count the money, and
then offer a prayer of thanks for all God's many blessings. Then
give the money away to a local charity to help some other family
experience some of God's abundant blessings from grateful hearts.

✠ Activity 41: The Lion, the Witch, and the Wardrobe

Every year my wife helps us clear out clothes for the thrift store.
Like Lucy, Edmund, Peter, and Susan in C. S. Lewis's classic tale
The Lion, the Witch, and the Wardrobe, we step into our wardrobes
only to find ourselves in a magic land on the other side. For Lucy,
the land is Narnia. For us, the land is Simplicity.

Our family has enjoyed many journeys to this new land. We've
come face to face with our own "White Witch" attitudes of greed,
selfishness, and ingratitude. There we've also met Aslan, the Great
Lion, who offers himself as a sacrifice. Through life with Aslan, we
are set free from a life of "always winter and never Christmas"[16]
and our stone statue hearts are melted into hearts of compassion.
The wardrobe in Lewis's story offers us a faith insight: our own
wardrobes of clothes have the power to transport us to mysterious
places of sacrifice, charity, and simplicity.

Through the Wardrobe

✠ In the winter, journey with your children into their wardrobe.

✠ Ask them to pick out any fall or winter clothes that do not
   fit anymore, or that they do not like to wear.

✤ Help them select clothes that haven't been worn for over a year.

✤ Collect all these clothes from each family member in boxes. As parents we need to model a willingness to give away our possessions, especially those we never use.

✤ Place the boxes of giveaway clothes in the family room at a family meeting.

✤ Encourage family members to tell a story about something relating to one piece of clothing they are giving away. One year, we took our giveaway clothes down to a mission church in Mexico. In that small Mexican village, later in the week, I saw a boy wearing our youngest son's favorite shirt he had outgrown. When I returned, I showed my son a photo of this Mexican boy wearing his shirt. Both boys were delighted with their gifts.

✤ Offer a prayer of thanks to God for the gift of clothing.

✤ Take the boxes to your local clothing charity store or drop-off location.

✤ Do the same in June with spring and summer clothes.

✤ Activity 42: Honeymoon Salad

Lettuce Alone.

—Recipe for making "Honeymoon Salad"

Parents get tired of parenting. Hostesses grow weary of providing hospitality. Even kids, with all their energy, have times when their energizer bunny stops beating on the drum and starts beat-

ing on their brother. Children and parents need time away from
each other.

Monasteries are places away from the "coming and going" of
busy humanity. Most of the monasteries I've visited are located
in the countryside, at the end of long driveways, far away from
freeways, shopping malls, and rush-hour life. The monks I know
have expressed their desire for even more solitude than most
Benedictine monasteries are able to offer.

Most monks spend more time together than most families. Besides three meals a day, monks also gather for five prayer services
and one Mass daily. On average, a monk meets together with all
the other monks seven times every twenty-four hours.

In all this coming and going to meetings, there grows a hunger for
more solitude. My wife and I serve in people professions. We spend
time with people all day. I love being with people. Yet my heart cries
out sometimes for time away from people. I get away every month
for a day of solitude, silence, study, and prayer. I go to a monastery.

In addition, my wife and I get away from our children one
day a week. We have the same day-off, and enjoy a day alone
together while our children are at school. This weekly gift has
been a saving grace for our marriage in times of difficulties. We
have the time and grace to quietly renew our life together away
from our children. Here are a few ideas for keeping your love life
fresh as honeymoon salad.

*Twenty-Five Creative Ways to Nurture Your Marriage
Apart from Kids*

 1. Light candles.

 2. Take a bath or shower together.

3. Read poetry to each other.

4. Sign up for a community college course together.

5. Go for walks to enjoy God's creation.

6. Spend time together in the garden.

7. Share your feelings with one another.

8. Write out lists of frustrations, tensions, stresses, and conflict issues: share them, pray over them, then burn them.

9. Tickle and laugh together.

10. Give a foot massage.

11. Watch birds.

12. Pack a picnic lunch. Hike to a beautiful spot and share a meal together.

13. Collect and press flowers.

14. Fold laundry together.

15. Go to garage sales or antique shops together.

16. Wash dishes together as you talk together about your day.

17. Every anniversary light a "Unity Candle" and recite your vows together. Light the same candle every time you forgive one another and make up after a fight.

18. Put on music and slow dance in the living room.

19. Write love letters to each other.

20. Read aloud to each other from a book you both choose.

21. Hold hands.

22. Cuddle.

23. Make love.

24. Enjoy morning devotions with coffee in bed.

25. Pray together.

✤ Activity 43: Enjoy Church Family Life

Recently, our family spent the day with a church volunteer work crew, planting a new garden in the church front yard. Thanks to a great local garden designer and a hard working volunteer crew, the new garden space welcomes people with grace and beauty. In years to come, our children will say, "I helped to plant that garden and look how beautiful it looks!"

The flowers of Benedictine spirituality unfold within a faith community. Benedict writes detailed instructions about receiving new members into the monastic community in chapter 58 of the Rule:

✤ *Novices should be clearly told all the hardships and difficulties that will lead to God.*

✤ *If they promise perseverance in stability, then after two months have elapsed let this rule be read straight through to them.*

✤ *After six months have passed, the rule is to be read to them, so that they may know what they are entering.*

✤ *If once more they stand firm, let four months go by, and then read this rule to them again.*

✤ *If after due reflection they promise to observe everything and to obey every command given them, let them then be received into the community.*

✤ *When they are received, they come before the whole community in the oratory and promise stability, fidelity to the monastic life, and obedience.*

Notice Benedict's emphasis upon reading the community Rule to new members three times over the period of a year. Four natural seasons go by while a new potential member of the community plants himself in the Rule. Benedict allows plenty of time for initial zealous emotions to wear off and the stability of root systems to grow.

One of our most important parenting tasks is planting and rooting our children within the family of faith, the church. Here are a few ideas to encourage parents in guiding our sons and daughters into God's faith community, the church.

Ways to Get Involved in a Local Church

✤ Nurture children in the faith from the beginning.

✤ Pray for children from the womb.

✤ Ask wise members of a local congregation to pray with you for your children.

✤ If you haven't ever prayed for your children, begin tonight to thank God for each child.

✤ Lead them with love into a relationship with God through Jesus Christ.

✤ Talk with them about God's family, the Body of Christ.

✤ Read stories of saints to your children.

✤ Go with them to Sunday School and to Sunday worship.

✤ Model the faith to your children through your active interest in faith and spiritual life.

✤ Have your children baptized.

✤ Tell them of the challenges in living a life of faith with God.

✤ Share with them your own spiritual struggles and joys.

✤ Let your children observe the growth in your life with God and with God's family.

✤ Instruct children in the faith.

✤ Volunteer with your children to help out around the church.

✤ Read Bible stories aloud to your children.

✤ Pray with your children and pray for your children.

✤ Allow spiritual grandparents to "adopt" your children and assist you in raising them in the faith.

✤ Take your children to other congregations and worship services. If possible, travel with your children to other countries and join with Christians in worship. In this way, your children will begin to see the bigger picture of the global family of God.

✤ When they are full-grown adults, let them leave and commit them into God's care

The bulbs our children planted in the new church garden in the front yard are already pushing their way up and will soon blossom. In the same way, as we plant spiritual bulbs in our children's lives, in God's good time they will blossom and become beautiful flowers within the family of faith.

✠ Activity 44: The Gift of Full Attention

Every month I drive two hours to a monastery where I spend the day in prayer and study. During this day away, I spend an hour with Father Tim Clark. Father Tim gives me a priceless gift: the gift of his full attention. I talk about my family, my work as a pastor of a local congregation, my spiritual life. Father Tim listens. He looks me in the eyes and says without words, "Your life is of great worth."

On one visit with Father Tim, I confided in him that I felt impotent to help people, especially those with deep problems. "I feel as though my words are empty," I confessed, "and I don't have anything to give to people." Father Tim smiled quietly, looked into my eyes and shared with me the wisdom of the cloister. "Just be fully present to people. That's all." "That's all?" I wasn't convinced. "That's enough," Father Tim reassured me. "Offer people a ministry of presence. In so doing, you act as Christ, who was fully present to us through the Incarnation."

I've been chewing on Father Tim's advice for a year now and it still hasn't lost its flavor. One of the greatest gifts we give our children is the gift of our full attention. The "ministry of presence" with children means taking time daily to "just be fully present" to our kids.

- ✠ **Get on their level.** With a baby, lie on the baby blanket and look eye to eye, fully present with this miracle of God. If you have young children, sit on the floor or in a chair at the same level as where they sit. Take an active interest in the music your teens listen to and listen with them to these songs and groups.

- ✠ **Learn the art of asking "open-ended" questions.** Ask questions that make your child the expert and you the learner. I love to ask our middle school son about life in middle school.

Open-ended questions do not have a "yes-or-no" answer. The answer is neither right nor wrong. Open-ended questions invite a person to share feelings, tell stories, and express ideas without fear of judgment or criticism.

✛ **Actively listen.** Open your ears, your mind, and your heart. Focus all your wandering attention upon this moment with your child. When distractions arise, set them gently aside and return your full attention to this precious gift sitting before you, the gift of your child.

✛ *Activity 45: The Family Treasure Chest*

For our oldest son's sixteenth birthday, I buried a treasure chest in the sand dunes near our house and sent him out on a treasure hunt to collect sixteen clues around our beach town. The sixteenth clue gave him the final piece of a treasure map, including an "X" that marked the spot where the treasure was buried. Earlier in the day I'd lowered an old footlocker filled with his presents into a pit I'd dug out in the dunes and covered it with sand. My son found all sixteen pieces of the treasure map, counted off the steps to the exact location in the dunes, and began to dig. After an hour he returned frustrated. No treasure chest. We looked together. Sure enough, right where I had buried several hundred dollars of birthday presents, including a new surfing wetsuit, there was no treasure and no footlocker. Pacing around, trying to figure out what happened, I stumbled upon some fresh digging in the dunes about twenty yards away. We dug there and to my great relief, he found the treasure. Someone had played a trick on us and moved the chest. Though the treasure had been obviously rifled through, nothing was stolen.

One of the great challenges families face today is something like a treasure hunt: the challenge of locating and digging up the great "treasures" buried by our parents, grandparents, and ancestors. I'm speaking of values, morals, and spiritual riches. How can we help our children discover their spiritual heritage? How do we assist our children to moral maturity? What values are we leaving as an inheritance to the next generation? Here are four ways to help our children discover their Family Treasure Chest.

1. **Spend time together.** Discover projects and activities in which both you and your children have a common interest. My dad worked with me for nearly a year refinishing a 1906 upright piano. We stripped off multiple layers of paint down to the bare wood. Adding several coats of a clear, natural finish revealed the rich beauty of the grain. We overhauled the action of the keys and reupholstered the bench. Then, best of all, we learned together how to play Ragtime piano. To this day, I can still remember the first section of Scott Joplin's "Maple Leaf Rag," thanks to Dad taking an active part in a project that interested us both.

2. **Talk together.** While you are together in your common project or activity, strike up conversation about values, morals, and spiritual life. I've discovered that children and youth are very interested in talking about matters of the heart when they are given the opportunity and the interest of an adult. Here are a few examples of questions and conversation starters from the piano refinishing project:

   ✦ What do you enjoy most about the piano?

   ✦ Tell me about the kind of music you like the most.

✛ Think about this old piano, built back in 1906: What do you suppose the world was like back then? How do you suppose it has changed since then?

✛ Pianos usually outlive the people who built them: What do you hope to leave behind when you die?

✛ Do you think there will be pianos in heaven? What about music in heaven?

3. **Actively listen.** Invite your children to freely share their views and values, even when you disagree with those views and values. Provide a nonjudgmental, safe harbor where your children can return again and again, tie up their lives, and truly be welcomed. Help your children grow in moral confidence and clarity through conversation about matters of the heart, including values, ethics, and spiritual life issues. Ask your children where they stand on moral issues using open-ended questions. Here is an example: "I'd love to hear what you believe about . . . ?" Then actively listen to your children's words, seeking to understand their mind and heart.

4. **Share your convictions.** We give our children a real treasure when we clearly mark out what we believe and value. I appreciate Rabbi Wayne Dosick's book *Golden Rules: The Ten Ethical Values Parents Need to Teach Their Children,* in which he encourages parents to write an ethical will. "No matter how much or how little you have," challenges Dosick, "you will probably write a will, leaving your possessions and your financial resources to your children. But you have something much greater and, ultimately, much more valuable to give your children. You can leave your children your ethical and spiritual legacy. . . . When you leave an ethical will, your

values will live on in your children, and your children will treasure your greatest gift."[17]

When we share our ethical and spiritual values with our children, it is like giving them a treasure map and inviting them to go check it out for themselves. Children love adventures. The "spiritual legacy" we leave our children is something like that treasure our sixteen-year-old son found on his birthday, a wetsuit. Not only will this gift help them survive the rough and tumble of the world in which we live; with this treasure our children will be equipped to help rescue others who were not so blessed to have grown up in a home with a family treasure chest.

Chapter Seven

ACTIVITIES FOR FAMILY GROWTH

So then, just as you received Christ Jesus as Lord, continue to live in him, rooted and built up in him, strengthened in the faith as your were taught, and overflowing with thankfulness.
                                                    —Colossians 2:6–7

When we moved into our newly built house in the forest on the north end of our village, we finally felt at home. We've transplanted our family six times, from rental home to rental home, through four states and nineteen years of family life. At last we've planted our roots in this new home.

To celebrate we replanted. We transplanted ferns from the surrounding forest. We planted gift rhododendrons, piggy-back plants, lilies, raspberry canes, and a dogwood tree. The excavators left a thirty-foot-wide swath of clay soil encircling our house. Into this soil we mixed good earth and planted new growing things. Winter is passing. Snowdrops have appeared under the Sitka spruce tree next to our new home. These first singers of spring are dwarfed by the old tree towering hundreds of feet above. Old

Grandfather Spruce has stood sentinel over this forest for over six centuries.

Some of Jesus' most loved stories involved fields, seeds, and growth. Jesus compared the Kingdom of God to seeds, crops, and trees. In one of his stories, some seeds fall upon hard soil and are snatched away by birds of the air. Some are sown among rocky soil. They spring up quickly but wither for lack of good roots. Other seeds perish before bearing flower or fruit, choked out by weeds and thorns. Finally, there are those seeds that fall upon good earth, bringing forth a bumper crop, even thirty-, sixty-, and a hundredfold.

Into the family field God continues to sow seeds of wisdom, seeds of truth, seeds of love. Every family field has hard soil, rocky places, weeds, and thorns. Every family also enjoys God's gift of good earth, soil that will bear fruit to eternal life.

The activities in this final chapter focus upon growth in the family cloister. Some of this growth happens in the midst of disappointments and hardships. Most of the growth in our family has happened in secret without much notice or fanfare. The presence of these seedlings of grace, wisdom, and love assures me of God's grace growing in our home through the seasons of family life.

✠ Activity 46: Doorkeeper of the Week

Given the opportunity, I'd go back to kindergarten in a heartbeat. I love the colors, the shapes, the smells, and the creativity of a kindergarten classroom. I love the way Robert Fulghum describes this priceless time of life in his *All I Really Need to Know I Learned in Kindergarten:*

Share everything.
Play fair.
Don't hit people.
Put things back where you found them.
Clean up your own mess.
Don't take things that aren't yours.
Say you're sorry when you hurt somebody.
Wash your hands before you eat. Flush.
Warm cookies and cold milk are good for you.[18]

In kindergarten, we learn how to get along with others outside our family. We learn to live in community. Someone gets to be responsible for being "line-leader" or "doorkeeper."

For fifteen hundred years, Benedict helped monks mature through sharing responsibility. One of the key shared responsibilities in the monastery is the doorkeeper. *At the door of the monastery, place a sensible person who knows how to take a message and deliver a reply, and whose wisdom keeps that person from roaming about* (RB, 66). Today, this person is called the Guestmaster.

Parents are wise to share responsibility with children, even from an early age. Children love being entrusted with a "big job." From their preschool years, we've tried to share with our children important "doorkeeping" tasks such as answering the phone, greeting people at the door, and discerning dangers. Following Benedict's instructions, here are a few ideas for family doorkeeping for a variety of ages of children.

Job Description for the Family Doorkeeper

✤ Learn how to lock and unlock all the doors in the house.

✤ Learn how to answer and hang up the phone.

✤ Learn sensible phone manners.

✤ Take phone messages and deliver them to the right person.

✤ Warmly receive guests who come to the door.

✤ Learn how to discern between unwanted strangers and welcomed guests.

✤ Check e-mail and notify family members of messages.

✤ Sort mail and deliver it to the family.

✤ Pass on messages and, if you have one, keep the message board up to date.

✤ Learn to be reliable and trustworthy through faithful service to others.

✤ Activity 47: Travel Games

"Let's play a game, Dad!" Our youngest son, Thomas, is usually the one to suggest travel games on a long road trip. Every year, we pack ourselves into a five-seat sedan, with our black Lab and three teenage sons and head out on a road trip: a camping vacation, a visit to family, or a sports competition with one of our sons. "You choose one we all can play, son." A travel game changes the whole environment of a cramped car into an entertainment center on wheels. The miles fly by unnoticed as we enter the battle of wits, humor, and observation.

Benedict wrote specific directions for monks who traveled away from the monastery (RB, 67). Though they were rooted in the vow of stability, Benedict assumed monks would go on occasional journeys and would require guidance for their travels. His guidance includes warnings about behavior outside the monastery, prayers for the departed monk, and welcome for travelers returning to the cloister.

When we travel we expose ourselves to dangers. Benedict was aware of these dangers in his day and prescribed specific guidelines for journeying monks. He also provided ways for the monastic family to remain united while members were away. As a family, we too offer our travel prayers and celebrate certain rituals that bind us together while we're traveling. Following the Benedictine tradition of uniting the family together during journey times, we pray and play while traveling in the car. One of our family rituals is playing travel games. Here are ten of our favorite travel games with directions how to play.

✤ **Categories:** (1) Players choose three categories (such as movies, cars, bodies of water, cities, countries, candy, toys, things you find at the beach). (2) One player selects a letter of the alphabet and tells the others. (3) All players think of items in each category which begin with that letter of the alphabet. (4) A player says, "Done!" when he has all his items. (5) All players share their items and keep track of points for each original item. (6) If any player has the same item as another, these items cancel one another out and no points are scored. (7) At the end of round one, have another player select a new letter of the alphabet for the next round. (8) Play ten rounds and see who is the category champ.

✤ **The Alphabet Game:** (1) Play two ways: Team or Individual. (2) Team: Everyone in the car looks outside the car for the letter "A." As soon as someone finds an "A," everyone looks for the letter "B." Continue through the alphabet until the "Z" is found. (3) Individual: Each person must find his or her own letter "A." When the first person finds an "A," all the others must still find their own "A." The winner is the first person to "Z."

✤ **I Spy!** One player, the Spy, looks outside the car, finds an object and declares, "I spy something _____" (describing the color or shape of the object). Other players try to guess what the Spy is looking at. Whoever guesses correctly becomes the Spy.

✤ **Twenty Questions:** (1) Choose a player to be the host. (2) The host chooses a real object. (3) The other players take turns guessing what the object is using only yes or no questions. (4) The players only get twenty questions or the host wins and chooses another object. (5) The first player to guess the object correctly becomes the host.

✤ **Three-Letter Challenge:** This game is best played between just two players. (1) Both players choose a three-letter word but keep it a secret from the other player. (2) Taking turns, players ask for letters. For example, "Does your word have the letter S?" (3) If they get a hit (correctly guess one of the letters), they get to ask for another. (4) Players may also use their turn asking if a letter is in a certain position. For example, "Is the letter S at the end of the word?" (5) The first player to correctly guess the other player's word is the winner.

✤ **License Plate Game:** See how many different license plates (states and countries) you can spot in one hour.

✤ **The Minister's Cat:** Going through the alphabet, players say, "The minister's cat is a _____ cat." Place in the blank a word beginning with the letter A. For example, "The minister's cat is an acrobatic cat." The second player must add a word beginning with the letter B. For example, "The Minister's cat is an acrobatic, beautiful cat." Keep adding adjectives until the players get to Z.

✤ **St. Peter:** This is a rhythm game with high potential to distract or annoy a driver, so get the driver's permission before starting. One player is named St. Peter. The other players are named "Number One," "Number Two," "Number Three," and so on until everyone has a name. St. Peter starts the rhythm by slowly tapping while she says, "St. Peter, St. Peter, St. Peter — Number One." Then the player who is named "Number One" must jump in without missing the beat and say "Number One — Number Two." Then the player who is named "Number Two" jumps in without missing the beat and says "Number Two — St. Peter." St. Peter now must respond back with "St. Peter — Number Three," and so on around the car. Players always say their name first; then they may call out any other name/number in the car. A player who messes up the rhythm of the beat or forgets to jump in must go to the end of the line. That player becomes the lowest number while all the other numbers move up one. Thus, if four people are playing and Number One messes up, he becomes Number Three, Number Three becomes Number Two, Number Two becomes Number One, and St. Peter stays St. Peter. The only way to oust St. Peter is to get her to mess up. St. Peter always sets the pace of the rhythm.

✤ **Cool Car Game:** See how many "Cool Cars" you can collect in one hour. Keep track by having someone be the "Car Lot," the person who writes down the color, make, and, if you can figure it out, the year of the car.

✣ **Car Dealer:** This game works best in an area with lots of cars and other types of vehicles. One player is chosen as the Car Dealer. The Car Dealer tells the players, "Look for a red sports car." The first person to spot a red sports car becomes the Car Dealer. Note: the Car Dealer does not have to have the intended car in sight when the round begins. He or she simply thinks up a type of vehicle and lets the players try to find one. One variation: the Car Dealer assigns a price tag for each type of vehicle. For example: "We're selling a silver car for $2,000 and a black semi-truck for $4,000." Have the Car Dealer just make up prices. They don't need to be what such a vehicle is actually worth. The first player to find a silver car adds $2,000 to her score and so on. We like to mix in easy cars (e.g., a white pickup truck) with the difficult (e.g., a police car with lights flashing). The first one to reach $100,000 dollars becomes the Car Dealer.

✣ Activity 48: The Trash King

Every Friday morning the Trash King arrives to receive our offerings to the Kingdom of Trash. We are his humble subjects doing our best. Our Trash Cache (the garbage can) overflows with our gratitude for the generosity of the Trash King, who weekly accepts our offerings. I dress up in my finest bathrobe and boots on Friday morning in anticipation of the Trash King's appearance.

Name anyone who enjoys taking out the trash. Benedict deals with the problem of undesirable tasks in chapter 68 of the Rule. He expects monks to accept such assignments *with complete gentleness and obedience*. With wise moderation, Benedict allows members of the community to bring their grievance or complaint to their superior with reasons why they cannot perform the task. A Benedictine community is not a place of slavery or forced labor. The goal is growth and maturity in Christ.[19]

Taking out the trash is one of the least favorite chores in our home. As subjects in the Kingdom of Trash, we have tried a variety of ways to get this task done *with complete gentleness and obedience*. Through a few regular trash-recycle rituals we've maintained good relations with the Trash King and helped our children grow up through faithful service and doing undesirable tasks. I offer below a modest review of our trash tasks with hopes that you know better how to serve the ever-gracious Trash King in your area through such simple acts of service.

Seven Ways to Honor the Trash King

1. Assign one child to be in charge of all the trash baskets in the whole house. Have this child empty these trash baskets at least once a week or as needed.

2. Set up a Recycle Center in your home. We use ten-gallon buckets and large trash cans to keep recyclables separate. We also have a recycle trash can in our utility room near the kitchen to collect these items through the week.

3. Every few weeks, we make a run to the Recycle Center in town. If you have a Recycle Queen in your area, invite her to come and pick up your items in her Royal Truck on a set schedule. We recycle all recyclable plastics, newspapers, magazines, bottles, cans, cardboard, greyboard, and plastic

bags. Find out what your community recycles and get going on this easy task.

4. Reuse items that can be used again without throwing them away after first use. One example: ziplock bags can be rinsed and reused several times. Bring your own grocery bags (cloth or canvas) to the market. We also save bottles with lids through the winter for summer canning.

5. Reduce your reliance upon highly packaged products that generate trash. Find creative ways to reduce your trash output. While you're at it, try to reduce your family energy consumption: electricity use, water use, fossil fuel use, and use of other natural resources. Try one of these reductions each month over a period of a year. Be gentle with your reductions, revealing to your family how you can get along with less when everyone works together.

6. Renew natural resources as possible. Once a year, plant a tree in your yard, neighborhood, or town. Compost your organic trash and return the good, composted earth to your yard.

7. Finally, offer the Trash King your gratitude. I know of a man in our village who sets out a love gift of a cold beverage for our garbage man (the Trash King) every week. When our Trash King arrives, I go out and exchange small talk for the few minutes he's there doing that royal task of receiving our trash tribute. Somehow, standing outside in my bathrobe and rubber boots watching the Trash King dump our offering into his big truck makes me feel grateful to simply be alive and smell the fragrance of another week gone by.

✠ Activity 49: Cutting Snowflakes

Snow seldom falls through the cedars in our beach village. Instead, we create our own snowstorm. Every year, beginning on the first of December, we cut snowflakes and put them up on every window of our home. This year, we cut "snowflakes" celebrating the Twelve Days of Christmas. We found a paper-cutting book with designs inspired by this traditional Christmas song. The "snow" doesn't melt until spring. We wait until the season of Lent to take down our snowflakes.

Benedict writes in the Rule of a common experience in every family, the *occasion of contention* (RB, 69). Families fight. People get cut and hurt. Sibling rivalry mixes with spousal tension. As Benedict handles the problem of family fights, *If any member assumes any power over those older or, even in regard to the young, flares up and treats them unreasonably, let that one be subjected to the discipline of the Rule* (RB, 70).

Conflict is normal even in healthy families. We are needy people. Our hearts are filled with a strange mix of fear and faith, regret and hope, harshness and kindness. One of the most effective ways in the family to defuse the *occasion of contention* is through creative expression, through a shared creative activity. In celebration of our uniqueness and frailty, try cutting snowflakes.

How to Cut Paper Snowflakes

✠ Provide scissors and white copy paper for every family member.

✠ Lay a plate or bowl onto a sheet of white copy paper and trace the circle.

✠ Cut out the circle.

✠ Fold in half and fold again into quarters.

✠ Following the diagram below, fold the quarter circle into thirds.

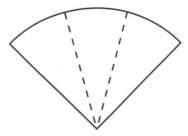

✠ You are ready to begin cutting your snowflake. Cut out designs from the sides, top, or bottom. For the snowflake to hold together, you simply need to leave a little edging on both sides of the wedge.

✠ After finishing your cutting, gently open your snowflake. Let your whole family see the fragile, beautiful, creative person you are. Tape your artwork to a window.

✠ Activity 50: The Cross on Our Wall

I've found a cross on the wall of every monastery guestroom. The cross is the first object I see when I wake up for morning devotions at a monastic prayer retreat, and the cross is the last thing I see before turning out the lights.

If you have spent any time in Christian churches, the cross is the central symbol you'll discover. Even the architecture of most Christian sanctuaries from the medieval period onward is cruciform, with a floor plan laid out in the shape of the cross.

Benedict centered his communal vision upon Christ and the cross. The Rule focuses upon the person of Christ and the love of Christ. Benedict's Christ-centered faith shines forth through such statements below found in the Rule.

Christ in the Rule of St. Benedict

We shall through patience share in the sufferings of Christ that we may deserve also to share in the eternal presence. (RB, prologue)

They [the abbot or prioress] are believed to hold the place of Christ in the monastery. (RB, 2)

Your way of acting should be different from the world's way, the love of Christ must come before all else. . . . Pray for your enemies for the love of Christ. (RB, 4)

The first step of humility is unhesitating obedience, which comes naturally to those who cherish Christ above all. (RB, 5)

We shall imitate by our actions that saying of Christ's: "I have come not to do my own will, but the will of the One who sent me." (RB, 7)

They are to imitate the loving example of Christ, the Good Shepherd, who left the ninety-nine sheep in the mountains and went in search of the one sheep that had strayed. So great was Christ's compassion for its weakness that "he mercifully placed it on his sacred shoulders" and so carried it back to the flock. (RB, 27)

Care of the sick must rank above and before all else so that they may truly be served as Christ who said: "I was sick and you visited me." (RB, 36)

All guests who present themselves are to be welcomed as Christ, who said: "I was a stranger and you welcomed me." (RB, 53)

Let them prefer nothing whatever to Christ and may Christ bring us all together to everlasting life. (RB, 72)

We have followed the monastic habit of marking our home with the sign of the cross. A cross hangs over our bed, between our marriage covenant vows. A friend brought us this cross from the Sacre Coeur (Sacred Heart) cathedral in Paris. It is my conviction that the cross is the sacred heart of the family. Only under the cross can our divisions, hurts, grievances, sins, and ills be healed.

Making a Cross for Your Home

Plan a "cross-making" activity as a family where family members are encouraged to make their own crosses.

✚ Make available a variety of tools and materials for this cross-making craft. Use wood, fabric, self-hardening clay, paper, paint, glue, wire, leaves, twigs, or other materials.

✚ Each family member writes out a Bible verse on a 3 x 5 card that expresses the meaning of the cross of Christ. Here are a few examples: Matthew 10:39; Mark 10:45; Luke 10:23; John 12:24; Romans 5:8; 1 Corinthians 1:18; 2 Corinthians 8:9; Galatians 2:20; Philippians 1:21; Hebrews 12:2.

✚ After the crosses have been crafted and verses written, hang them up together in your home, over your front door, in your living room, over your bed, in your kitchen. Place them in places where you will be daily reminded as a family of God's forgiveness, love, and power to heal us through Jesus Christ.

✠ Activity 51: Poetry Night

Every year we attend the "Fisher Poets Gathering" held in Astoria, Oregon, in February. Jon Broderick, a good friend and a commercial fisherman in Bristol Bay, Alaska, started this celebration a few years ago. I love hearing poetry written and read by working men and women. The family of commercial fishermen welcomes a large crowd of land-based locals, and we celebrate the fishing industry together in verse and song. I've asked myself, why not plan such an event every year for a cluster of families in a neighborhood? Here's how it might happen.

✠ Gather several families together for an evening of poetry.

✠ Collect poems from books of poetry from your local library, your church library, or the Bible.

✠ Together with your children, pick out a few poems you like and mark them.

✠ Rehearse these poems with your children.

✠ Set up a room in a home with a stage area and an audience area.

✠ In the stage area, place a chair, a good reading light, and books of poetry.

✠ Have each family bring poems to read and refreshments.

✠ Encourage every family member to take the stage and read a poem aloud.

✠ If you have prereaders, have them echo after you a simple, children's poem.

✤ After each reading, the audience claps and shares what they like about that poem.

✤ Include in your poetry night any poems written by members of the family.

✤ Before the poetry night, invite families to write a poem about themes of faith and love. Here are few themes from Benedict's Rule, chapter 72, which could be used as titles of poems your family writes about faith and love in the family:

Good zeal which leads to God and everlasting life.

Fervent love.

Show respect to the other.

Supporting with greatest patience one another's weaknesses.

Earnestly competing in obedience to one another.

Show pure love.

Prefer nothing whatever to Christ.

May Christ bring us all together to everlasting life.

✤ Activity 52: Family Hiking

We love to hike as a family. Every year we find a few old trails to discover anew. We've hiked beaches with newborns in a front pack. We've hiked mountain trails with toddlers and preschoolers. We've hiked together through the preteen years and right into the heart of that strange and wondrous land called adolescence.

Along Eagle Creek trail in the Columbia Gorge, just thirty miles upriver from Portland, Oregon, we hiked one hot summer day up to Punchbowl Falls. The trail steadily climbs up and up, getting higher and more dangerous the further you hike. We kept a close eye on our children along this trail with no guardrails. Several miles up, another trail splits off and leads back down into the narrow valley to Punchbowl Falls.

After enjoying our picnic lunch along Eagle Creek, our family climbed aboard a thirty-foot log in the creek and paddled, like Robinson Crusoe, upriver to the falls. Surrounded by ferns, moss, and mist, Punchbowl Falls evokes a longing for Eden. What a wonder of God's grace to sit as a family in the middle of such a natural paradise, drinking in the goodness and refreshment of God's creation.

Even the miserable hikes have offered our family a shared memory and the confidence to weather rain, cold, and adverse conditions. One hike started south along the Oregon coast into fifty-mile-per-hour winds. After just a hundred yards trudging along the beach into a cold, stiff wind, we went back to the car, drove south ten miles and hiked north with the wind at our back. A disaster turned into a delight!

Like Eagle Creek trail, the family journey keeps going up, increasing in difficulty and danger. But the scenery also increases in beauty and glory. No matter how old or young, we keep a close eye on our children. Together, through each of the switchbacks and surprises in the trail, we grow a little stronger and hopefully a little wiser.

Are you journeying as a family toward your heavenly home? With Christ's help, I hope this little "toolbox" of family activities, inspired by the Rule of St. Benedict, written by a beginner for beginners, may encourage you in your journey together as a family. I love the way Benedict concludes the Rule. He describes our family life as a journey home, up into the mountains of God's love.

Are you hastening toward your heavenly home?
Then with Christ's help, keep this little rule that we have written
*   for beginners.*
After that, you can set out for the loftier summits
of the teaching and virtues we mentioned above,
and under God's protection you will reach them. Amen. (RB, 73)

Epilogue

WRITING YOUR OWN FAMILY RULE

A few years ago, a teacher friend called to apologize for neglecting to invite me to the annual educator banquet in our local school district. She told me I had been selected to receive a "Friend of Educators" award and had been honored at the banquet the night before. I thanked her for saving me from embarrassment. We laughed about it, and she brought by a lovely glass sculpture representing this award. Into the thick glass someone engraved the words of an African proverb, "It takes a whole village to raise a child." I've placed it in my window where I work, allowing the morning light to shine through the proverb.

Benedict knew that spiritual maturity came from small steps of faith taken together. He would have loved that African proverb. In the early sixth century, he called together a little village of monks and offered them a little guidebook for their common life together, the Rule.

In Benedictine monasteries around the world over the past fifteen hundred years, millions of spiritual children have been raised together into faith maturity.

The family as designed by God is intended to be a place of spiritual growth. We will continue to grow in our family as we welcome the wisdom of others who have walked before us. I encourage parents to write this wisdom down, to craft your own Family Rule, drawing upon the wisdom of God through the Scriptures, saints, and contemporary sages.

Writing Your Family Rule

✤ Meet together with a few other adults over several weeks or several months.

✤ At each meeting: read, study, write, discuss, and pray.

✤ Read from wise books on parenting and family life. Read together from the Bible about God's way of family life and love.

✤ Study: dig into Scripture and wise books describing community life, parenting, and spiritual growth.

✤ Write: keep a journal of the wisdom shared in the group. Log into this journal the trouble areas, challenges, and questions you have during the week as they arise.

✤ Discuss: talk together frankly about the difficulties and joys of parenting. Ask questions of one another. Sharpen one another in the exchange of perspectives. "As iron sharpens iron, so one man sharpens another" (Proverbs 27:19).

✤ Pray: Ask God's guidance and wisdom to direct you as parents in this process of writing a Family Rule.

✤ After these meetings together, sit together with your family to write your Family Rule. Share your parenting journal with your children, according to their age and ability to understand.

✤ Organize your Family Rule under headings. Try using the categories from *The Family Cloister:* Family Design, Family Spirituality, Family Discipline, Family Health, Family Life Together, Family Hospitality, and Family Growth.

✤ Under each of these headings, write out principles and approaches to family life, the guidelines that all will strive to follow.

✤ Write into your Family Rule verses from the Bible that will guide your life together.

✤ Listen carefully to your children and include their wisdom and insights in your common life together.

✤ After several family meetings, where you all work together on your Family Rule, choose one member of the family to compose a rough draft. Read this aloud at the next family meeting.

✤ Make any changes, amendments, additions, or corrections. The goal is to write a gracious, flexible handbook for practical spiritual living as a family.

✤ Once you've written the final draft, present this aloud to the entire family.

✤ Pray as a family, committing your Family Rule to the Lord.

✤ At least once a year, reread your Family Rule aloud at a family meeting.

✤ Make any changes, and once again, through prayer, commit your family life to the *path of God's commandments.*

✤ As Benedict encourages us in his Family Rule:

Do not be daunted immediately by fear,
and run away from the road that leads to salvation.
It is bound to be narrow at the outset.
But as we progress in this way of life and in faith,
we shall run on the path of God's commandments,
our hearts overflowing
with the inexpressible delight of love. (RB, Prologue)

NOTES

1. Quotations from the Rule are italicized throughout the text.

2. David Robinson, *The Family Cloister: Benedictine Wisdom for the Home* (New York: Crossroad Publishing Company, 2000).

3. Thomas Merton, *New Seeds of Contemplation* (New York: New Directions, 1962), 72.

4. Robinson, *The Family Cloister*, 18.

5. Ibid., 33–35.

6. Eleanor H. Porter, *Pollyanna* (New York: Scholastic, 1987), 31–32.

7. William Kilpatrick, *Books That Build Character: A Guide to Teaching Your Child Moral Values through Stories* (New York: Touchstone, 1994).

8. See Robinson, *The Family Cloister*, 188.

9. Robert Frost, from *Frost: The Poet and His Poetry* (New York: Bantam, 1967), 105.

10. This quotation was found at www.gardeningbythebook.com. Marjorie Waters's book *The Victory Garden Kids' Book* (Old Saybrook, Conn.: Globe Pequot Press, 1994) is currently out-of-print.

11. I am indebted to Robert Burns and his book *Self-Growth in Families: Kinetic Family Drawings* (New York, New York: Brunner/Mazel Publishers, 1982) for the concept of family portraits. While I offer this activity as a creative family event, Burns offers it as a professional therapeutic tool for "measuring family dynamics." Most parents are not professional therapists. I am grateful for the rise of marriage and family therapy, available in most cities in our country today. As a pastor, I encourage parents to seek professional counsel in times of family crises and in the midst of ongoing family troubles.

12. Gerard Manley Hopkins, from *The Poems of Gerard Manley Hopkins* (Oxford: Oxford University Press, 1967), 66.

13. Shel Silverstein, *Where the Sidewalk Ends* (New York: HarperCollins Publishers, 1974), 19.

14. *A Child's Book of Prayers* (New York: Henry Holt & Co., 1985), 23.

15. Hugh Feiss, O.S.B., *Essential Monastic Wisdom* (New York: HarperCollins, 1999), 55.

16. C. S. Lewis, *The Lion, the Witch, and the Wardrobe* (New York: Macmillan Company, 1950), 14.

17. Wayne Dosick, *Golden Rules: The Ten Ethical Values Parents Need to Teach Their Children* (New York: HarperCollins, 1995), 194.

18. Robert Fulghum, *All I Really Need to Know I Learned in Kindergarten* (New York: Villard Books, 1988), 6.

19. See Robinson, *The Family Cloister*, 174.